# Contents

Quiz Answers on page 110

Blue Peter

# Hello!

IT MAY FEEL LIKE WE SAY THIS EVERY YEAR, BUT THE PAST TWELVE MONTHS REALLY HAVE FELT LIKE SOME OF THE MOST EXTRAORDINARY WE'VE EVER HAD!

From kayaking down the Amazon to meeting Miley Cyrus on the set of Hannah Montana. From racing trucks at Brands Hatch to rowing across the English Channel. From JLS performing in the studio to toppling a whole load of mattresses around BBC TV Centre.

And from time to time, just when we think that week's shows might not be quite up to scratch, something else new and amazing and crazy and inspiring comes along for us to tell you about. Like a man who plays bass guitar on balloons. Trust us, you had to see it to believe it!

So for this Annual, we've taken all the best bits, squeezed out anything that's even remotely boring, and jammed all the remaining highlights into these 112 pages.

We really hope you enjoy it. Tell us what you like and what you don't. We want to know, because right now, we're working on more new stuff for the next few months. And we want it to be even better...

Helen
x x

# ...AND THANK YOU!

Jodie

Jacob and Benjamin

Simon

Eleanor and Rosalind

Emma

Daniel

Tarun

We love having a go at amazing things - but we love it even more when you get involved too.

We adored the brilliant gowns you designed for our Send a Smile appeal. The pictures and messages you sent to inspire us on our ultimate challenges really made all the difference.

And every single day we get hundreds of emails, letters and photos telling us everything from what you've been up to, to when you've had a go at our makes and bakes.

The best win Blue Peter badges, of course. Which isn't just a piece of history, but also gets you free entry into over 200 badge attractions around the UK. So go on - why don't you give it a go?

EVERYTHING YOU NEED TO KNOW ABOUT THE BADGES IS ON PAGE 80.

## GET IN TOUCH!
Web: bbc.co.uk/bluepeter
Email: bluepeter@bbc.co.uk
Post: Blue Peter, BBC TV Centre, London W12 7RJ

# CONGRATULATIONS

## HUGE? MASSIVE?! OUR COMPETITIONS ARE SO BIG, THESE TWO AMAZING WINNERS ARE MAKING HISTORY!

### Royal Mint 50p comp

This is the first time that a child anywhere in the world has designed a coin that's become legal currency. And that honour has gone to 9-year-old Florence, with her brilliant drawing of a pole vaulter.

We ran the competition with the 2012 London Olympics and the Royal Mint (all the UK's coins). Four million of her 50ps will be made, so hopefully you can put one in your money box very soon.

Florence with Andy, gold medal-winner Denise Lewis, and her new coin

### Dr Who Tardis Console comp

This is an absolute cracker!

This competition was all about designing a Tard console that will get and feature in a futu episode of Doctor W We had thousands o entries, featuring everything from pinba machines as date gener to fishtanks as time rotors.

But Matt Smith, the new Do loved the imaginative detail 12-year-old Susannah from Lancashire's entry, and nan her the overall winner. Exp see her console in an episo Doctor Who in 2011.

Well done Susannah!

## Watch out for more competitions on the show so

# BRAIN-PUMPING BLUE PETER

BRILLIANTLY-PUZZLING, BOLDLY-PERPLEXING, BODY-POPPING BLUE PETER. WELL, MAYBE NOT BODY POPPING, BUT THE REST ISN'T FAR WRONG WITH THIS QUIZ OF THE YEAR'S HIGHLIGHTS.

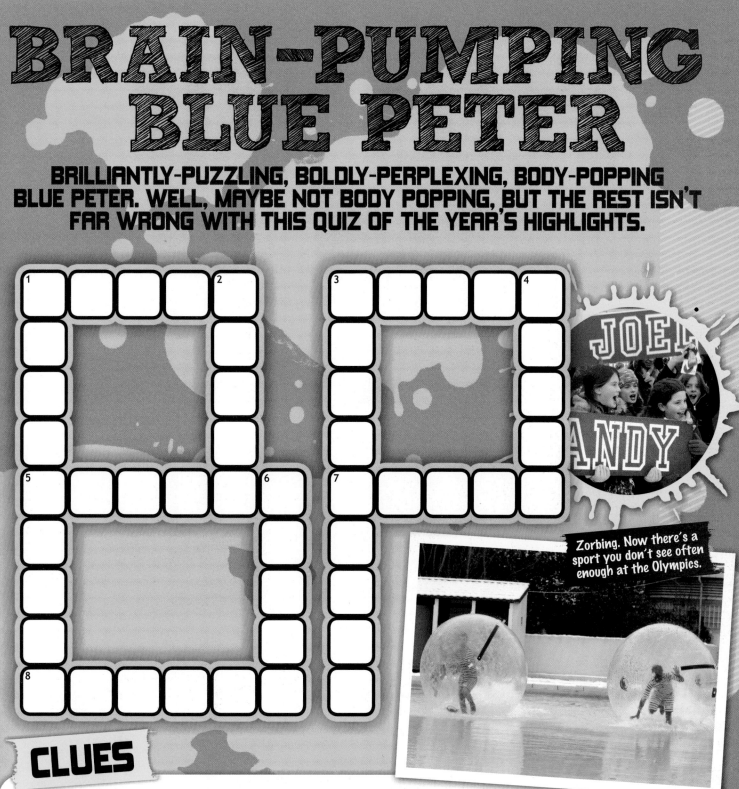

Zorbing. Now there's a sport you don't see often enough at the Olympics.

## CLUES

### ACROSS:
1) Brands -----, the race track where Andy raced (and crashed!) his truck
3) We said goodbye to this furry friend after 14 years as a Blue Peter pet
5) What colour was the camper van that took us across Turkey?
7) The surname of the actor who plays Doctor Who, who's appeared several times on the show
8) A type of medical expert who was with Helen throughout her Amazon adventure

### DOWN:
1) What's the famous US film-making town which Joel visited during his acting adventure?
2) We say this at the start of every programme!
3) The first name of the actor who plays Doctor Who (see clue 7 across)
4) A little black blood-sucking creature which Joel tried out during our Gruesome Great Britain week
6) We went zorbing on this blue, wet liquid in one of our craziest challenges (see photos)
7) Send a -----, the name of our appeal

THE ANSWERS ARE ON PAGE 110.

# 10 THINGS YOU DIDN'T KNOW ABOUT Helen

**1** My earliest memory is going to watch my brother be a mascot at a football match, and all the players wiggled their hips as they did their warm-up. I found it hilarious! But then I promptly fell asleep during the match. I was three at the time and I don't know if the memory is vivid because I remember it, or because everyone else has been telling me it ever since.

**2** All my family are football mad. My grandad is 87 but he still has the same seat at Carlisle United's ground, Brunton Park.

**3** One of my mum's favourite sayings is "Only boring people say boring".

**4** My flat is a complete tip! It looks like a department store has thrown up in there.

**5** If I could be in any film it would be the Peter Pan film, Hook. I'd love to be Tinkerbell, simply because it'd be great to be able to fly everywhere.

**6** On my days off I love to walk the dog. Or go on a bike ride. Anything to clear my head and get some space.

**7** Other jobs I've had include working in a sweetshop, being a waitress and presenting a breakfast programme on local radio. I'm a qualified tap dance teacher, and I was once an extra on Coronation Street when I was at college.

**8** My favourite joke is: What do you call a man with a seagull on his head? Cliff.

**9** One of my favourite teachers at school was Mr Connell. He was my history teacher. He really loved what he did and he loved old museums and everything. I loved the fact that he loved his subject.

**10** I adored growing up in the countryside. There was so much space that you could hit a golf ball from the back doorstep. But I also love living in the city now. There is so much going on and you can just go out and do and see whatever you want.

One of my toughest challenges: street dancing, with champion dancer Akai as my mentor.

Helen's recent challenges include kayaking down the Amazon, learning streetdance and surfing. What challenge do you think Helen should take on next?

# TARDIS BIRD FEEDER

THE NEW DOCTOR WHO, MATT SMITH, POPPED IN TO THE BLUE PETER GARDEN TO HELP ME MAKE THIS: A BIRD FEEDER THAT LOOKS LIKE HIS VERY OWN TRAVELLING TIME-MACHINE. IT TAKES A BIT LONGER THAN SOME OF OUR MAKES, BUT IT'S WORTH IT. AND WHAT'S A FEW EXTRA MINUTES TO A TIME LORD?!

## You will need:

- 2-litre juice carton
- 1-litre juice carton
- Sticky tape
- String
- PVA glue
- Thick cardboard
- White and blue paint
- Sports bottle cap

## STAGE 1

Use the 2-litre juice carton to create the main Tardis. Clean and dry it, then open up the top and cut down each of the four corners.

## STAGE 2

Fold these corners out and you'll have four flaps. Cut off the flap with the pouring hole in it.

## STAGE 3

Fold the three remaining flaps over to make a flat top and tape them all down. Make a hole in the middle and thread some string through it. This is what you'll hang up the Tardis bird feeder with. Tie a knot in the string inside the Tardis and stick it down with tape, so the string doesn't come through.

# MAKE IT

## STAGE 4

Now, make the top of the Tardis by getting the 1-litre juice carton and cutting off the bottom 5cm.

## STAGE 5

Cut 2cm up each corner and bend the sides out to create four flaps. Make a hole in the middle of the cut-off bottom, and thread your string through it. Stick this cut-off bottom on the top of the main Tardis carton with tape.

**Either my Tardis has shrunk - or I've grown!**

13

## STAGE 6

Cut out a square hole in the middle of one of the sides. Make it big enough for birds to get in and get the bird seed inside. Then get some cardboard and cut out shapes to give the raised effect on the rest of the sides. Stick the cardboard on with glue and paint the whole thing white.

## STAGE 7

Now you can paint the whole thing blue!

## STAGE 8

Complete the look by decorating your Tardis. Print out these authentic designs from the Blue Peter website, or photocopy this page four times and cut them out and stick them on. Then do one final coat of PVA glue all over to make it weatherproof. Finish it off by getting a sports bottle cap, making a hole in it, and threading it onto the string to create the light.

## STAGE 9

Fill your birdfeeder with bird seed or leftover food and hang it in the garden, in a yard, on a balcony or in a time vortex in a completely different galaxy. Your choice.

## DID YOU KNOW?

- The Tardis is the Doctor's personal time-travelling machine.
- Tardis stands for Time and Relative Dimension in Space
- The Tardis appeared in the very first episode of Doctor Who back in 1963.
- It was based on the look of a police box, which back then was a very common sight in UK towns and cities.
- Police boxes had a telephone inside, so that – in an age before mobile phones or police radios – officers could call their police station when they were out and about.
- Members of the public could also use it to call the police station in an emergency
- When the light on top flashed, that meant a police officer needed to call the station urgently!

POLICE PUBLIC CALL BOX

POLICE PUBLIC CALL BOX

POLICE TELEPHONE
**FREE**
FOR USE OF
**PUBLIC**
ADVICE & ASSISTANCE
OBTAINABLE IMMEDIATELY

OFFICER & CARS
RESPOND TO ALL CALLS

**PULL TO OPEN**

# FINDERS KEEPERS

## Clothing Conundrum

THE BADGE COMES WITH US EVERYWHERE! BUT CAN YOU GUESS WHICH PRESENTER IS WEARING THE BADGE IN THESE PHOTOS?

## Team Talk

WE'VE HIDDEN THE NAMES OF ALL THE PRESENTERS AND PETS IN THIS SNEAKY LITTLE WORD SEARCH. CAN YOU FIND THEM ALL - AND WORK OUT WHICH PET ISN'T IN THE LIST?

```
L E B A M H Y S
D L U C L E O J
U S O B Q L V Y
C O O K I E X E
S C A Y R N U N
F K M N B T S R
Y S U P D W L A
N T L U C Y E B
```

HELEN    ANDY    JOEL

SOCKS    COOKIE    BARNEY

LUCK    MABEL

The missing pet is:

THE ANSWERS ARE ON PAGE 110.

15

# FUNKY LUNCHES

DAD MARK NORTHEAST COULDN'T GET HIS SON TO EAT HIS LUNCH, SO HE CREATED FUNKY SANDWICHES OF EVERYONE FROM HARRY HILL TO SHAUN THE SHEEP AND OUCHO. WE GOT HIM TO TURN COOKIE INTO A SANDWICH - AND HERE'S HOW YOU CAN DO IT AT HOME TOO.

## You will need:

- 2 slices of white bread
- 1 slice of brown bread
- A cucumber
- A red apple
- Butter
- Spring onion (optional)

What have they done to me? Get my agent!

# BAKE IT

## STEP 1

Make Cookie's ears by cutting out small triangles of brown bread. Spread butter on the underside to glue them to a slice of white bread.

## STEP 2

Cut out a shape that's a bit like a sideways "B" from your brown bread. Glue that, again using the butter, to your white bread.

## STEP 3

Now cut out a triangle from your second slice of white bread. Glue that into the gap in the middle of your brown "B".

## STEP 4

Make Cookie's eyes by cutting out thin slices of cucumber and glueing those to the middle of the "B". Finish them off with thin slices of dark green cucumber skin.

## STEP 5

Make Cookie's nose by cutting out a small triangle of red apple skin and glue that in position.

## STEP 6

Now create Cookie's whiskers by cutting out thin slices of cucumber skin or slicing up a spring onion, and glue those in position.

## AND FINALLY

Show your mum how clever you've been by eating (and enjoying!) your yummy Cookie sandwich!

Clever thinking by Rebecca, who took the ideas here and created a Sandwich Shelley. A badge for you, Rebecca! ☺

# HELEN'S AMAZING AMAZON ADVENTURE

## HOW I KAYAKED OVER 2,000 MILES AND SMASHED TWO WORLD RECORDS!

## MY CHALLENGE

Almerim

Nauta

To become the first woman in history to kayak solo along the Amazon: a total distance of 2,010 miles.

START: Near Nauta, where two rivers join to form the Amazon proper.

END: Near Almerim, where the Amazon becomes tidal.

## PREPARATION

I suppose I've got a bit of a reputation for taking on huge challenges. Last year's 78-mile triple-marathon in Namibia for starters.

But when I decided to kayak down the Amazon for Sport Relief, I knew this would be my biggest challenge ever. Not least because I had only two months to fit in a lifetime of training.

First off, I had to learn how to kayak. Then I spent a couple of full days on the river to build up my strength and stamina.

The intial signs were encouraging. But by the time I flew to South America, whether I'd cope with kayaking 10 hours a day, six days a week, for six weeks - well that was a complete unknown!

I'm up for it!

Before I began, I spent time in Peru, meeting some of the children who could be helped by Sport Relief. Nine-year-old Henry doesn't go to school. Instead, every day he hunts through this massive rubbish dump to find bits of metal, which he sells to recycling firms for a few pence. It's a terrible existence, and I knew that if I encouraged even a few more people to raise money for Sport Relief, my adventure would be worth it.

## DID YOU KNOW

The Amazon is the world's biggest river. There's more water in the Amazon than the next ten largest rivers put together.

## THE START

JANUARY

20

And so we arrive at the banks of the Amazon. The biggest river in the world, just in case anyone needs reminding!

Stuart (The Cameraman)

Eric (The Director, who ran the trip)

Gavin (The Soundman)

Even getting to this point has meant endless battles with permits, equipment and local officials. And 24 hours before I'm due to start live on air on Blue Peter, we find out that our main support boat, the Spectrum, is delayed. There's a huge question mark over whether I'll be to get underway at all, and I'm reduced to tears.

1 mile down. 2,009 to go...

But my amazing crew pull various cats out of various bags (so to speak), not least by hiring a different support boat for two days. We're good to go! So we hook up our portable satellite link, my face appears on BBC One, I wave at Joel and Andy, get into my kayak - and make the first of more than one million strokes.

The official entry in our log book – to prove it's all real!

20 WEDNESDAY Start: S04 26'87'5 W098 27'14'2 DAY 1
Distance: 32.3m / 51.2km
End GPS: S04 09'77'2 W07 3'15'59'6
Weather: Cloudy, Hot
Start/End Time: 12:00pm / 4:30p.
Footage: En Route
Start
First thoughts
WITNESS!
MAX: 7.2k / 11.7km.

## DISASTER STRIKES...ALREADY!

**JANUARY 21**

I know it's going to be tough – but I don't expect to hit problems only on day two! In the extreme heat, my hands suffer from the non-stop kayaking, and blisters look inevitable. Fortunately, Lucy, our doctor has a solution. She tapes up my fingers, something we'll now have to do every day for the next six weeks.

**JANUARY 28**

I'm pushing myself hard to reach my target of 60 miles a day. It's led to bouts of tears, aches and exhaustion, but so far I'm on track. Then, today, we hit an obstacle which I've got no control over. We're crossing the border between Peru and Brazil when we discover extra paperwork checks that no one told us about. Eventually we make it across, but altogether I lose a day's kayaking. I'm feeling the pressure and it's stressing me out.

NOT my most flattering photo ever, but the worry shows through.

## DID YOU KNOW

More than 20% of all the world's river water is in the Amazon.

**JANUARY 30**

My worst day so far. The border incident freaked me out and I'm determined to keep going whatever. In the morning I do a huge 50 miles. But in the afternoon, amid 38-degree temperatures, I feel sick and suddenly have to come off the river. My head hurts and Lucy has to inject me twice in the bum. She tells me I have heat exhaustion. I just think I'm going to die.

I just feel so... weak.

# HALFWAY THERE!

After the heat exhaustion shock, I realise I have to do things differently. So I start going out earlier (5am!) and finishing later (anything up to 9pm). Crucially, this means I can take a bit more time off for lunch during the heat of the day.

Some days are better than others. Once, I got hit by the heat again and only did 45 miles. That day I hated my kayak for the first time. Other times, I feel like I'm making real progress.

## DID YOU KNOW

More than half the world's estimated 10 million species live in the Amazon.

Reading the messages you sent makes all the difference in the world. I cannot tell you how flattered, humbled and grateful they make me feel. I read them on the Spectrum, and think about them in those long, lonely hours in the kayak.

I'm closer to the end than the beginning!

The crew on our support boat, the Spectrum.

1000 MILES

FEBRUARY
7

And then, on 7 February, a milestone I thought I might never see. One thousand miles - a huge distance, and halfway there! The crew celebrate, but to be honest, I don't. It's only day 19, and I know anything could still wreck my challenge. I don't want to start taking it easy.

# ULTIMATE CHALLENGE!
# HELEN'S AMAZING AMAZON ADVENTURE

## MORE DRAMAS

**FEBRUARY 8**

Nothing on this adventure is straightforward! There's me, thinking I'm making progress, and suddenly we discover that we've got to get to the city of Manaus two days earlier than planned, to complete more paperwork ahead of some bank holidays. I have to up my target to an exhausting 70 miles a day for the next week.

**FEBRUARY 13**

Thanks to fast currents, cooler temperatures, and probably the fact that I'm getting better at this thing, unbelievably we get to Manaus on schedule. And then it's on to one of the most amazing sights anywhere on this river. The "Meeting of the Waters" is where a darker, thicker and warmer river, the Rio Negro, joins the muddier and faster Amazon. For about six miles, the two rivers run side-by-side, till they eventually mix.

**FEBRUARY 16**

Possibly the biggest disaster of the whole trip! For a few scary hours I think my whole kayaking adventure might be off. Overnight, our safety boat is hit by a freak wave and sinks. All morning the crew try everything to pull it out, but nothing seems to work. At last, they get it high enough to empty out the water. And just when I think it's sorted, we discover that my kayak got cracked too. Fortunately we have some fibreglass resin to repair it, but once again we're behind schedule. Once again I end up in tears in my cabin.

C'mon guys, you're doing great!

## ⊗ DID YOU KNOW

There are no bridges anywhere across the Amazon.

# HEADING FOR THE FINISH!

I've always found that, though the last stretch of a challenge is just as hard physically as the opening, it often feels easier. It's like the final marathon I ran in Namibia last year, which went by like a breeze.

**ANNE-MARIE**

The Amazon is the same. The river is as wide as a sea, and at times it's exhaustingly choppy, but because I know the end is in sight, the final week seems to race past. Even when a sick bug spreads through the rest of the crew, miraculously, I'm spared.

**FINISH**

**Don't run me over!**

**Yeesss! I've done it!**

## FEBRUARY 28

And then, after nearly six incredible weeks, the day I've been waiting for. Sunday 28 February. At exactly 1.53pm, with tens of thousands of people watching at home live on the BBC News Channel, I cross the finish line to cheers and fireworks. I'm exhausted and ecstatic.

We paddled 2,010 miles down the world's biggest river! I say "we" because I only got over that finish line with your support. There were days when I was sick, tired and stiff, but I knew how many of you were willing me on, and I didn't want to come back and have to make some excuse for not finishing.

THANK YOU SO MUCH FOR YOUR KIND WORDS AND YOUR THOUGHTS - I OWE YOU. SO ONE QUESTION. WHAT NEXT?!

# HELEN'S AMAZING AMAZON ADVENTURE

## WHAT EVERYDAY LIFE WAS LIKE

Here's me on the deck of the Spectrum, catching up on just a few of the amazing good luck messages you posted on the Blue Peter website.

One of the cabins we slept in. I'd normally be in bed by 9pm ready for my early starts!

In our planning room, we kept a chart to show how much progress I was making – to make sure I never slipped behind.

The cook taking delivery of some fresh fish for our meals.

The cook taking deliver.... No, OK, this we could never eat! It's a huge catfish caught by a local fisherman.

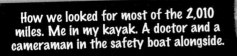

How we looked for most of the 2,010 miles. Me in my kayak. A doctor and a cameraman in the safety boat alongside.

Along the way, I got glimpses of the mighty rainforest through which the Amazon flows.

It was amazing seeing how ordinary Amazonians live. In the wet season, this area is flooded so these stilts become the pathways.

Amazingly, I managed to break two Guinness World Records: the longest solo journey by kayak, and the longest distance in a kayak in 24 hours by a woman. Even now, I still can't really believe it...!

# PUZZLED PETS

## SHELL-SHOCKED SHELLEY

OUR TORTOISE SHELLEY IS TIRED OF HER GREEN SHELL. AFTER ALL, SHE'S BEEN LIVING WITH IT FOR OVER 20 YEARS! CAN YOU COLOUR HER IN AND GIVE HER A BRAND-NEW LOOK? THE BRIGHTER THE BETTER!

What's the name of your pet?

..............................

Which is your favourite Blue Peter pet?

..............................

## BOWLED OVER

THE BLUE PETER PETS' BOWLS HAVE BEEN SCRAMBLED UP BY A MISCHIEVOUS JOEL. CAN YOU UNSCRAMBLE THEIR NAMES SO THEY KNOW WHICH ONE TO EAT FROM? AND WHICH PET'S BOWL HAS GONE MISSING?

1. SKOCS

__ __ __ __ __

2. EYLLESH

__ __ __ __ __ __ __

3. RAYBEN

__ __ __ __ __ __

4. CULY

__ __ __ __

THE PET WHOSE BOWL IS MISSING IS: _____

26

# TAKE THE LEAD

POOR BARNEY, MABEL AND LUCY! THEY'RE GOING CRAZY TO GET OUTSIDE, BUT THEIR LEADS HAVE GOT ALL TANGLED UP. CAN YOU WORK OUT WHICH PRESENTER IS HOLDING WHICH LEAD, SO THEY CAN GET OUT AND GO FOR THEIR WALKIES?

HELEN

JOEL

ANDY

Which animal would you love to have as a pet?

......................

LUCY

BARNEY

MABEL

# TRUE OR FALSE

YUM YUM! SOCKS AND COOKIE HAVE MUNCHED AWAY AT THIS TASTY PIECE OF FISH, BUT IT'S REVEALED A WHOLE LOAD OF QUESTIONS. DO YOU KNOW WHETHER THEY'RE TRUE OR FALSE?

True or False

Socks is a Ragdoll cat

Socks likes getting his teeth cleaned

Socks lives in Devon

Cookie hates baths

Cookie is female

Cookie's best friend is Socks

ANSWERS ON PAGE 110

27

# PERSONALITY PROFILES

## How well do you know the Blue Peter presenters?

Being a Blue Peter presenter is a full-time job, but we do have a *bit* of time to relax.
So what do we get up to? See if you can guess which presenter has which profile!

### PROFILE 1

Favourite film Ratatouille
Top TV show Big Babies
Dream car Raleigh single-speed bike (not a car!)
Best sport Football
Ideal pet Piglet
Fave item of clothing
Jean shorts
Worst subject Science
Worst food Capers
Best time of day Night-time
Favourite artist Big Boi
Dream holiday destination
India
Phone Blackberry
Best day of the week Friday

**WHOSE PROFILE?**

### PROFILE 2

Favourite film Toy Story 3
Top TV show Being N-Dubz
Dream car Mercedes SLK 500
Best sport Football
Ideal pet Cricket
Fave item of clothing
TOMS shoes
Worst subject Woodwork
Worst food Snails
Best time of day 7am
Favourite artist Ellie Goulding
Dream holiday destination
South Africa
Phone iPhone
Best day of the week
Saturday

**WHOSE PROFILE?**

### PROFILE 3

Favourite film
The Shawshank Redemption
Top TV show Friends
Dream car Jaguar E-type
Best sport Hockey
Ideal pet Dog
Fave item of clothing
Leather jacket
Worst subject Maths
Worst food Curry
Best time of day Early - 6am
Favourite artist Lily Allen
Dream holiday destination
Greek Islands
Phone Blackberry
Best day of the week Friday

**WHOSE PROFILE?**

ANSWERS ON PAGE 110.

# QUICK CHALLENGE

# GIANT CHESS

1. When a huge chess board came to London's famous Trafalgar Square, I was determined to have a go myself.

2. And there was only one opponent I wanted to play. One of the UK's best young players, and already a world chess champion: 12-year-old Emma Bentley.

**Can you give me any sneaky tips?**

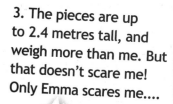

**I can't do that - you're my opponent!**

3. The pieces are up to 2.4 metres tall, and weigh more than me. But that doesn't scare me! Only Emma scares me....

4. So we took our sides and started the match. I decided to copy her every move. I thought it would work. I was wrong.

**If I hide here, she might not see me!**

5. Despite some cunning moves, she beat me easily within just half an hour. But at least I lasted longer than her quickest victory: 30 seconds.

6. I wasn't sure what the biggest thing was I'd met that day: those giant chess pieces, or Emma's skill!

**DID YOU KNOW?** Each side of the board is 8 metres long!

# CELEB GUEST:
# JUSTIN BIEBER

## TOP STATS
**Full name:**
Justin Drew Bieber
**Job:** R'n'B singer
**Main home:**
Atlanta, USA

## QUICKFIRE QUESTIONS

**How did you become famous so young?**

"I was about twelve-years-old and was in a singing competition. It was just a bit of fun - I was at home and my parents recorded it and put it online and the whole thing just happened so fast."

**What was it like meeting US President Barack Obama?**

"I got the honour to perform for him and his wife. It was such a great opportunity."

## TRUE OR FALSE?

**1.** The music manager who spotted videos of Justin performing on the Internet is called Scooter Braun

☐ **TRUE** ☐ **FALSE**

**2.** Soon after he was spotted, Justin got star help from US pop/rap legend Vanilla Ice.

☐ **TRUE** ☐ **FALSE**

**3.** When he was young, Justin taught himself to play the drums, piano, guitar and trumpet.

☐ **TRUE** ☐ **FALSE**

## KEY DATES

**1 March 1994:** Born in Ontario in Canada. **17 November 2009:** Released first album, My World. **24 January 2010:** His single Baby, with Ludacris, hits number 3 in the UK charts. **23 March 2010:** Released second album, My World 2.0. Entered the US charts at number one.

**ANSWERS: 1 and 3 are true; 2 is false. Justin in fact had a meeting with R'n'B star Usher.**

## TOP STATS
**Full name:**
Jack the Lad Swing
**Job:** R'n'B boy band
**Main home:**
London, UK

## KEY DATES

**18 March 1985:** Marvin Richard James Humes is born in London.
**7 December 1986:** Jonathan Benjamin Gill is born in London.
**27 November 1986:** Oritsé Williams is born in London.
**13 February 1988:** Aston Ian Merrygold is born in Peterborough.
**13 December 2008:** JLS are runners-up to Alexandra Burke in The X Factor **19 July 2009:** Beat Again is the first of two JLS singles to go to Number One that year.

## QUICKFIRE QUESTIONS

**If you hadn't been popular as singers, what would you have done?**
*Aston:* "Footballer." *Oritse:* "I think I would have tried to be a Blue Peter presenter." *Marvin:* "Probably a T-shirt designer." *JB:* "I would have been a doctor."

**Who is the smelliest of the group?**
*All:* "Marvin." *Marvin:* "No!"

## TRUE OR FALSE?

**1.** JB takes the longest to get ready before a photoshoot.

☐ **TRUE** ☐ **FALSE**

**2.** When he was younger, Aston starred as Cookie in CITV's Fun Song Factory.

☐ **TRUE** ☐ **FALSE**

**3.** In February 2010, JLS became the first former X-Factor contestants to win a Brit Award (and they actually won two).

☐ **TRUE** ☐ **FALSE**

37    37a    38

# GREATEST OUTFITS RATED

IT WOULDN'T BE BLUE PETER IF WE DIDN'T DRESS UP, SO FEEL FREE TO SNIGGER AT OUR MOST RIDICULOUS COSTUMES.

## 1920s

**What is it?** The kind of get-up that early skiers would have worn

| AUTHENTICITY: 6 | PRACTICALITY: 4 |
|---|---|
| FASHION FACTOR: 5 | SILLINESS: 9 |

**Why we wore it:** To tell the story of how winter sports were invented, as part of our "Winter Rivals" challenges.

**Did you know?** A British skier, Arnold Lunn, helped invent modern skiing, creating the first slalom race in 1922 and holding the first world downhill championships in 1931.

## NEOLITHIC

**What is it?** Clothes from 9,000 years ago

| AUTHENTICITY: 5 | PRACTICALITY: 1 |
|---|---|
| FASHION FACTOR: 4 | SILLINESS: 8 |

**Why we wore it:** So we could recreate life in a Neolithic city during our expedition to Turkey (see pages 104-109)

**Did you know?** We were the first people ever to try to spend a whole night in a recreated Neolithic-style hut in Çatalhöyük. (We got smoked out and failed.)

## VICTORIAN

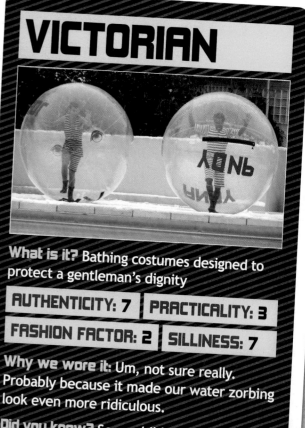

**What is it?** Bathing costumes designed to protect a gentleman's dignity

| AUTHENTICITY: 7 | PRACTICALITY: 3 |
|---|---|
| FASHION FACTOR: 2 | SILLINESS: 7 |

**Why we wore it:** Um, not sure really. Probably because it made our water zorbing look even more ridiculous.

**Did you know?** Some children in Britain are using these water balls to keep fit. Apparently, all you need is a 5-minute workout!

# ORIGAMI

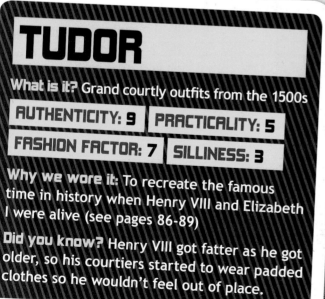

**What is it?** A dress made out of 1,000 paper cranes

| AUTHENTICITY: 3 | PRACTICALITY: 1 |
|---|---|
| FASHION FACTOR: 10 | SILLINESS: 4 |

**Why we wore it:** Because we thought it looked absolutely amazing - and it was made by a 16-year-old girl, Yuliya Krypo.

**Did you know?** In Japan, a crane is a holy creature, and an ancient legend says that folding 1,000 origami paper cranes will make your wish come true.

# MORRIS DANCER

**What is it?** A traditional English folk dance outfit

| AUTHENTICITY: 7 | PRACTICALITY: 5 |
|---|---|
| FASHION FACTOR: 1 | SILLINESS: 9 |

**Why we wore it:** Because Joel loves dressing up? Actually, so he could make lots of noise and charm worms. Don't ask...

**Did you know?** Morris dancing is at risk of dying out because, according to reports, young people aren't willing to give it a go.

# TUDOR

**What is it?** Grand courtly outfits from the 1500s

| AUTHENTICITY: 9 | PRACTICALITY: 5 |
|---|---|
| FASHION FACTOR: 7 | SILLINESS: 3 |

**Why we wore it:** To recreate the famous time in history when Henry VIII and Elizabeth I were alive (see pages 86-89)

**Did you know?** Henry VIII got fatter as he got older, so his courtiers started to wear padded clothes so he wouldn't feel out of place.

# BARNEY JOINS BLUE PETER

## THE FULL STORY OF HOW OUR FAVOURITE NEW PET JOINED THE SHOW

Me and my brother Gavin on our farm.

Ever since I was a little girl growing up on a farm, I've been surrounded by animals. Since I moved to London to present on CBBC, I've loved living in a city - but I've not liked not having a four-legged friend.

Of course, we have Lucy and Mabel, who we love loads. But as you may know, they don't live with us, so we only see them when we're in the studio.

So I nagged and nagged and nagged my boss, the programme's editor, to let me have a dog who could also join Blue Peter.

It wasn't an easy decision. We had to think about what we'd do when I went on filming trips. I had to be sure that I would always put his needs first.

I was helped by animal charity Dogs Trust. They analysed what I do, to see if it was OK to have a dog, and what sort would suit me best. They would also help me with another of my aims: to adopt an abandoned dog.

So we thought about it, and talked about it, and worked things out. And eventually we had a decision. I could get a dog! Yay! So I started my hunt for my new pet.

## HELEN'S STORY

That's a lot of travelling you do!

34

Barney

By Mairi

# BARNEY'S STORY

Barney and his brother Beanie were found wandering alone and abandoned in a village in Ireland. No one knows exactly when they were born, but our best guess is February 2009.

A friendly person took them to a local rescue centre, and when no one claimed them, they were moved to a Dogs Trust rehoming centre in West London.

The centre manager, Richard, immediately took a shine to Barney, who seemed very relaxed and wanted to be everybody's friend. He was easy to train, and especially liked being with children. Richard knew that I was looking for a dog, and so he kept a special eye on Barney.

I really wanted to see all the dogs rehomed!

Both Beanie and McGregor have gone to good homes too!

## HOW WE MET
Finally the time came for me to visit the Dogs Trust centre. I saw all kinds of wonderful animals, but Richard had identified two that would be particularly suitable for me: Barney, and a brown-and-white spaniel puppy called McGregor.

They were both so adorable. McGregor was super-sparky: running around and always wanting to play! Barney was quite different: unbelievably cute and affectionate, preferring to lick me and have his tummy tickled.

In the end, what's most important is a dog that is suitable for your life. McGregor was younger than Barney and I was concerned about having such a bouncy puppy. And I just loved Barney's wonderful temperament and the fact that he was so good with children. The decision was made.

By Dominic

# STARTING WORK

Barney getting used to my home!

That summer, I made sure that Barney and I got to know each other really well. I spent a lot of time with him, in the park and at home.

And then, at last, it was time for Barney to appear in the Blue Peter studio. I was so excited as I knew he was about to be unveiled to the millions of you who watch the show!

The day went brilliantly. Barney was really friendly with Joel and Andy, and spent time with Lucy and Mabel. He got a bit tired, and seemed to spend quite a bit of time chilling out on the computer desk. But thanks to your reaction afterwards in emails and letters, we know his first TV appearance went down a treat.

Uh-oh, he's been sick again! ↓

By April

# HOW BARNEY'S GETTING ON NOW

When Barney joined Blue Peter, he was quite young and there were still some training issues to iron out. He liked to eat food from the office bins, for instance.

But the biggest issue was that he got really travel sick in the car. We tried all sorts of methods, including ideas that you sent in. In the end, reassuring him that all would be well and making him feel secure proved to be the best method.

Since then, Barney's got on famously (which is appropriate, for one of the most famous dogs in the UK!). He loves coming on filming shoots. He is very happy in the studio. And if I can't take him travelling, he sometimes goes to stay at my mum and dad's farm in Cumbria. He loves all the space and having other animals around.

Barney is a very happy dog. I love seeing the pictures which you send in. He loves the attention. And most of all, we're a team, which is what all good dogs and their owners should be.

Barney with a filming camera on his collar.

Does my bum look big in this?

# 10 THINGS YOU DIDN'T KNOW ABOUT

# Andy

**1** My mum and dad currently live in Florida, but they've lived all over the world. They were born and grew up in Nigeria, but they've also lived in the UK, France, Japan, Italy and Germany. They've settled in Florida because they need the sunshine!

**2** I've only lived in two countries: Nigeria and the UK. I moved here when I was eight and lived in Birmingham till I moved to London.

**3** When I dream, I often dream that I can fly. I'm always being chased by people and I fly away, but then I slowly come back down and then I wake up because I've fallen to the ground.

**4** I love scarves. I have got loads and loads of scarves.

**5** The best present I ever got was a Batmobile remote control car from my mum. The remote control was actually attached to the car by a wire, but I still loved it.

One of my proudest achievements: running 150m just 4 seconds slower than Usain Bolt.

**6** I once appeared on Ready Steady Cook!

**7** I absolutely adore photography. I go out all the time just taking photos, and I'm fascinated by people. I was at the beach during the summer, and photographed this guy who was wearing massive headphones and walking along with two dogs. He just really looked out of place.

**8** I would love to be a great actor. I think that's the ultimate skill: to be able to pretend to be someone else.

**9** One of my elder brothers is an entertainer on a cruise ship. He told me recently he wants to be a TV presenter, so I'd better give him some advice!

**10** If there was somewhere I could go, it would be to the North Pole. I found out recently that a black man, Matthew Henson, was probably the first person ever to stand on the North Pole, in 1909. He was the assistant of the man leading the expedition, but he actually got there first. I never knew that. That's cool.

**Andy's recent challenges include truck racing, sprinting and extreme pogoing.**
What challenge do you think Andy should take on next?

# EASY EASTER BUNNIES

WE LOVE SUPER-FAST MAKES. WE RECKON THAT WITH A BIT OF PRACTICE YOU COULD DO THIS IN LESS THAN 60 SECONDS. WHEN EASTER COMES AROUND, THIS IS THE PERFECT WAY TO GIVE SOMEONE A LITTLE CHOCOLATEY PRESENT.

## You will need:
- A flannel ● Elastic band
- Googly eyes ● Felt
- Cotton wool
- Double-sided sticky tape
- A chocolate egg!

# MAKE IT

## STAGE 1

Get your flannel and fold it in half diagonally.

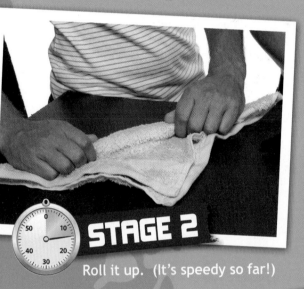

## STAGE 2

Roll it up.  (It's speedy so far!)

**Hurry up Joel!**

## STAGE 3

Bend your flannel "sausage" in half.

## STAGE 4

Fold the ends back to make ears and then put an elastic band over your new fold to create the bunny's head.

## STAGE 5

Decorate it!  Stick on eyes and a felt nose using double-sided sticky tape.  Add a tail using cotton wool.

## STAGE 6

Then put your egg in, and hey presto, you're done! Not even a minute!

## DID YOU KNOW?

- At Easter, Christians celebrate Jesus coming back to life after dying on the cross.
- Bunnies and eggs are linked with Easter because they also celebrate new life.
- Easter moves every year. Easter Sunday is always the first Sunday after the first full moon after 21 March. Complicated, eh?!

# SPOT THE DIFFERENCE!

**WELL, FOR A START, WE'RE NOT IN THE STUDIO. THIS IS WHEN WE WERE IN THE BLUE PETER GARDEN AHEAD OF THE WORLD CUP. THAT ASIDE, SEE IF YOU CAN SPOT THE TEN DIFFERENCES BETWEEN THE TOP AND BOTTOM PHOTOS.**

**PS:** Obviously, if this was Spot the Ball, rather than Spot the Difference, then you'd have no problem! But in fact, that's a very famous ball that Joel is holding. It's the actual ball that England played with when they won the 1966 World Cup Final. It's now kept at the National Football Museum in Preston.

ANSWERS ON PAGE 110

# GOLD BADGE
# Word Search

## WILL YOU SHINE IN THIS GOLD-PLATED QUIZ?!

The Blue Peter Gold Badge is rare and incredibly special. We give out only a few every year! We award them to amazing children who've saved a life or raised thousands for charity, and to famous people who've represented their country, inspired children, or done something to make children's lives better.

See if you can find all these Gold Badge winners in this special wordsearch. (And as an extra quiz, do you know who all the people are? Compare your answers with the right ones on page 110…)

```
T L E W I S H A M I L T O N
G J U I N X H J B D Q Z S G
J K O G G A R Y B A R L O W
T R R U Z P D B O N C E V F
V O T E N R A O D I F N E X
E W M S F M V A D H T N B J
R L L D Q K I Z T A O Y O T
I E Z A I D G J R U H K
N B R A L B L V M K E A
G Q S T H E Q U E E N W
Z P E R C Y T R N R
  M Q T K Z Y O U Y
  K J D H K D L H
    P L A A V Y
      B M I C
        R N
```

### GARY BARLOW
is not only a member of Take That, but he also organised the Comic Relief celebrity climb to the top of Mount Kilimanjaro, which raised millions for charity.

- DANI HARMER
- DAVID BECKHAM
- GARY BARLOW
- LENNY HENRY
- LEWIS HAMILTON
- MADONNA
- JK ROWLING
- THE QUEEN
- TOM DALEY

## THE SOLUTION IS ON PAGE 110.

# WHOOPIE PIES

WE'RE PROUD TO SAY: WE HELPED DISCOVER WHOOPIE PIES! WE WERE THE FIRST PEOPLE ON BRITISH TV TO SHOW YOU HOW TO MAKE THESE AMERICAN INVENTIONS. NOW YOU CAN BUY THEM IN LOTS OF PLACES - BUT IT'S STILL MORE FUN TO MAKE THEM YOURSELF.

## You will need:

- 80g margarine or butter
- 100g brown sugar
- 1 egg
- 20g unsweetened cocoa
- 200g all-purpose flour
- 1 teaspoon baking powder
- 1 teaspoon bicarbonate of soda
- A pinch of salt
- 1 teaspoon pure vanilla extract
- 100ml milk
- Marshmallow fluff or squirty cream
- Cream and sprinkles for decoration
- 3 mixing bowls
- Whisk

For once, Helen's worse at this than me!

## STEP 1

In your first bowl, mix the butter, sugar and egg.

## STEP 2

In your second bowl, mix the cocoa, flour, baking powder, soda and salt.

## BAKE IT

## STEP 3

In your third bowl, mix the vanilla extract and milk.

## STEP 4

Now get your first bowl (the butter mixture) and whisk in some of the second bowl (the dry mixture).

## STEP 5

Add a bit of the third bowl (the milk mixture) to the first bowl, and whisk again. Repeat steps 4 and 5 until all the ingredients are mixed together and the mixture is smooth.

## STEP 6

Drop spoons of the mixture onto greased baking sheets. Bake in the oven at 350°F or 160°C for 10 to 15 minutes.

## DID YOU KNOW?

- Whoopie pies were invented in America in the rural Amish community.

- They were designed as cake sandwiches that workers could have in their lunch boxes and wouldn't break up or get messy.

- They got their name because – apparently – when the Amish men found them in their lunchboxes, they were so excited, they went "Whoooppeeeee!"

Why not make some as a Mother's Day present?

## STEP 7

When the cakes are completely cool, take two at a time and stick them together using marshmallow fluff or cream as a filling. Then decorate them in any way you like!

# ANDY'S TRUCK RACING ADRENALINE RUSH!

## Ultimate Challenge!

BLUE PETER

60

ANDY

DAF

**Do I want to have a go? Of course!**

**It's completely mad!**

## CAN I BEAT MY NERVES AND RACE AGAINST PROFESSIONALS IN A HIGH-SPEED TRUCK RACE?

Those crazy producers at Blue Peter manage to scour the earth and find the most extreme and dangerous things for us to do. But I'm not complaining!

When we found out about truck racing, a totally insane motor sport where people race 5-tonne lorry cabs at speeds of up to 100 mph, I just knew I had to have a go.

My challenge was to take part in a professional truck race at top racing circuit Brands Hatch. And I had only a few weeks to prepare!

The truck even visited the studio, so Helen and Joel could check it out!

And I've caused the most almighty pile-up!

My final position: 12th out of 20. Not bad for a beginner!

That was amazing - nothing can beat that adrenaline!

But I'm a fighter - I start the engine again, and get back in the race.

On the final lap, I'm even starting to overtake again.

Back in the studio, my racing champion mentor Stuart Oliver gave me a first-time achievement award.

That's brilliant, I've absolutely loved it - thank you!

RESULT!!!!

**START**

**01** **02**

Your first disguise is rumbled. Rubbish! Go back to the start.

**04** **05** **06** **07**

You don't see th handover from your fellow spy Miss a turn.

# SPY CHASE!
## MOUSTACHES, MAPS AND MURDEROUS MANHUNTS!

COULD YOU CUT IT AS A REAL-LIFE SPY? WE TESTED OUR UNDERCOVER SKILLS WITH THE GUYS AT MI HIGH, SO WHY DON'T YOU TOO? GET YOUR FRIENDS, SOME DICE, AND SEE WHO MAKES IT TO THE END FIRST.

You get to your briefing and concentrate hard. Roll again.

**10** **09**

**12**

**14** **13**

**15**

Bypass the security systems. Go forward six spaces.

ACCESS GRANTED

**17**

**18**

**19**

## How to play

Your top-secret mission is to collect a tape and deliver it to Oscar. Use coins or counters to represent Joel, Andy or Helen (or Carrie and Rose too). Youngest goes first. Roll your dice and follow the instructions. No cheating. Oh - it's about spying. And spies double-cross. But still no cheating. Cheating's just annoying.

**24** **25**

**23**

These sunglasses are a bit dark, aren't they?

**20**

**21**

Your camouflage isn't good enough and you get spotted. Go back six spaces.

50

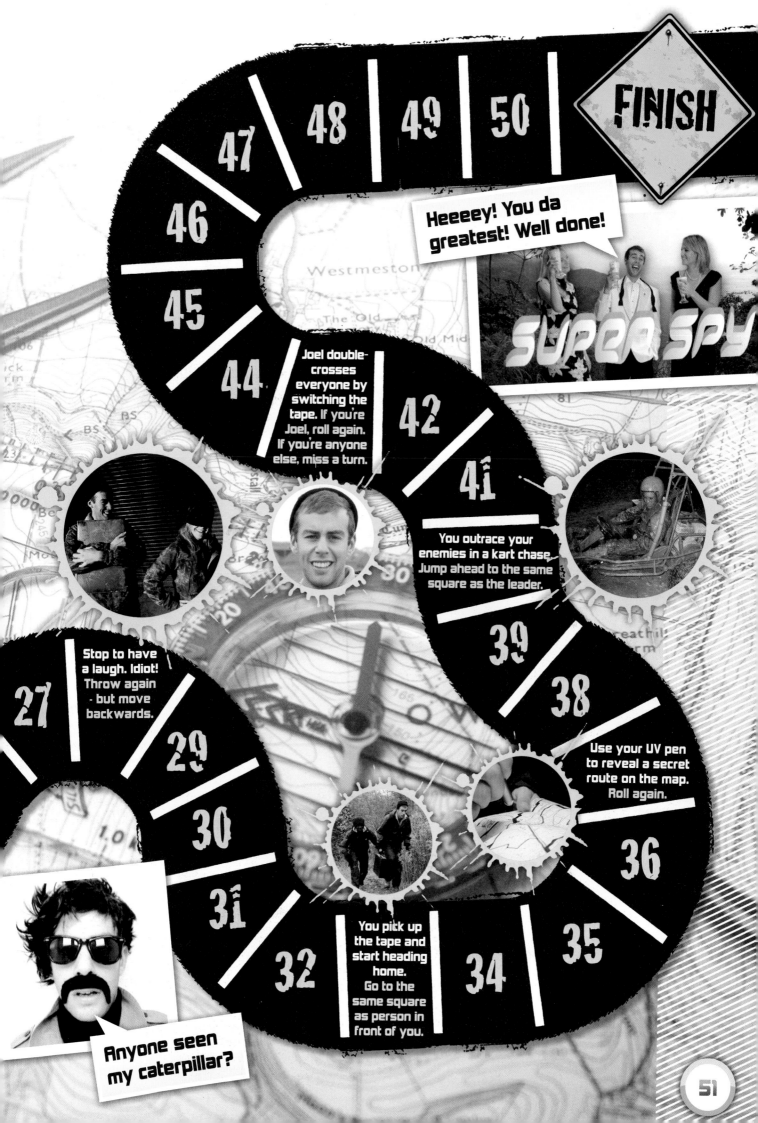

FINISH

47
48
49
50
46
45
44

Joel double-crosses everyone by switching the tape. If you're Joel, roll again. If you're anyone else, miss a turn.

42
41

You outrace your enemies in a kart chase. Jump ahead to the same square as the leader.

Heeeey! You da greatest! Well done!

SUPER SPY

39
38

Use your UV pen to reveal a secret route on the map. Roll again.

Stop to have a laugh. Idiot! Throw again - but move backwards.

27
29
30
31
32

You pick up the tape and start heading home. Go to the same square as person in front of you.

34
35
36

Anyone seen my caterpillar?

# MATTRESS DOMINOES!

## CAN WE SMASH THE WORLD RECORD FOR ONE OF THE WORLD'S CRAZIEST SPORTS?!

### 4.34pm

One minute till we're broadcasting live on BBC One. 100 volunteers standing by. The world-famous circular "donut" at BBC Television Centre about to witness what could be one of the most spectacular stunts in its history. But why on earth are we doing all this?!

### 6 weeks earlier

The idea of using bed mattresses as human dominoes was actually invented by American students in the 1970s. But not many people had heard of it until a UK bed company decided to have a go with 41 mattresses. The video of their attempt spread like wildfire on the Internet, so we decided to go one better. Well, 59 better, to be precise.

### That morning

Weeks of preparation start to become reality when 100 mattresses arrive outside our studio at TV Centre. We'd done some experiments to find the ideal distance between them, and marked up white lines on the floor to show where they should go.

**1.45pm**

The volunteers start to arrive...

**2.20pm**

The first of many tests takes place...

**4.05pm**

With all going well, the silly costumes come out...

# AND THEN WE'RE ON AIR!

Joel sounds the horn, and Helen, on the first mattress, falls backwards. She knocks over the man behind her. The person behind him goes down too. It's all starting to work - and it goes so fast too. Within 45 seconds we've completed the donut circle. The line of mattresses goes inside, toppling all the time, and ends up in our studio. Andy, on the final, 100th, mattress, falls over. We've broken the world record! It's another legendary moment on Blue Peter!

**GUINNESS WORLD RECORDS**

**CERTIFICATE**

The world record for the largest human mattress dominoes is 100 people achieved by **Blue Peter** at BBC Television Centre, London, United Kingdom, on 22 September 2009

GUINNESS WORLD RECORDS LTD

# WE DID IT!

# DRAW YOUR OWN LOGO!

## How to draw Blue Peter - the easy way!

Lots of you send in drawings of the Blue Peter logo - but how to get it right? Help is at hand with this easy-to-use grid. Just copy the design into the squares below and colour it in.

**TOP TIP:**
Why not copy the grid in pencil onto a sheet of A4 paper? Make the side of each square 3cm long and it will fit nicely onto the page. When you've finished, just rub out the pencil lines.

# QUICK CHALLENGE

# THRONE CLEANER

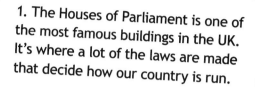

Oh I say, it's dirty here!

1. The Houses of Parliament is one of the most famous buildings in the UK. It's where a lot of the laws are made that decide how our country is run.

2. And every year it's host to a rather famous visitor: the Queen. She sits in a throne and give a speech which says what new laws will be passed over the next year.

3. Today, it's host to someone a bit less famous: me. I've been given exclusive access... to do a bit of cleaning!

4. But not just any old cleaning. Oh no. I've come armed with a special vacuum cleaner to clean the Queen's throne, which hasn't had a proper brush-up in years.

Now where DID Joel leave his chewing gum?

5. I have to be incredibly careful, as this intricate and beautiful piece of golden furniture was built way back in 1847, and has been sat on by six different Kings and Queens.

6. I'm even told to use a bit of spit on a paintbrush to get rid of the toughest stains. Apparently that really is the best method. Let's hope Her Majesty appreciates it when she sits on it a bit later!

## DID YOU KNOW?
The event is officially called the "State Opening of Parliament"

# CELEB GUEST:
# SELENA GOMEZ

## TOP STATS
**Full name:** Selena Marie Gomez
**Job:** Actress and singer
**Main home:** Los Angeles, USA

## QUICKFIRE QUESTIONS

**What's been the funniest moment on the set of Wizards of Waverly Place?**

"The boys who play my brothers are huge pranksters, so they do things I cannot stand! One time they got toilet paper and completely trashed my dressing room. But they're like my brothers, so although I get annoyed, we're all just a big family and we do things like that to each other all the time."

**What are your goals and dreams for the future?**

"I feel that I have been very lucky so far already. As to the future, I just want to heighten what I'm doing, and be the best I can be at everything."

## TRUE OR FALSE?

1. Selena does a huge amount of charity work, and is the youngest Unicef ambassador ever.

☐ TRUE ☐ FALSE

2. She was named after a Country and Western singer from Nashville called Selena.

☐ TRUE ☐ FALSE

3. She met her best friend Demi Lovato at the auditions for Barney & Friends.

☐ TRUE ☐ FALSE

## KEY DATES

**22 July 1992:** Born in Texas, USA. **1999:** Begins her acting career aged 7 on US children's TV show Barney & Friends. **12 October 2007:** Wizards of Waverly Place, starring Selena, premieres on the Disney Channel. **29 September 2009:** Selena and her band release their debut album, Kiss & Tell.

ANSWERS: 1 and 3 are true; 2 is false. She was named after a Tejano (Spanish Texan) singer called Selena.

# ROWING

**What is it?** Using oars to push a boat along water

| DIFFICULTY: 7 | DANGER: 6 |
|---|---|
| COST: 7 | FUN: 3 |

**What Joel did:** Rowed (as part of a team) across the English Channel. It took him 11 hours to cover the 35 miles.

**Did you know?** The first known rowing races took place on the River Thames in London. One race, Doggett's Coat and Badge, started in 1715 and still happens each year.

# ROLLER DERBY

**What is it?** A full contact sport between two teams competing on roller skates.

| DIFFICULTY: 6 | DANGER: 8 |
|---|---|
| COST: 4 | FUN: 7 |

**What Helen did:** Playing as "Helen Hard as Nails", she joined a UK roller derby team and played in a whole match, scoring several points as her team's "jammer".

**Did you know?** Roller Derby is normally played by women aged 18 and over, and has a strong "punk" feel with lots of make-up - as well as lots of pushing and shoving.

# ICE KARTING

**What is it?** The latest winter craze: driving motorised karts across ice rinks.

| DIFFICULTY: 3 | DANGER: 8 |
|---|---|
| COST: 8 | FUN: 10 |

**What Andy and Joel did:** They competed in a series of ice karting races for the Winter Rivals series. Andy won. (Joel can't drive!)

**Did you know?** The kart grips the ice using specially-developed studded tyres, which allow you to do all kind of stunts, from controlled skids to serious steering.

# BEAT THE DEADLINE!

If you've ever sat through movie credits, you'll know that a huge number of people work behind-the-scenes. It's pretty similar on Blue Peter. The show may be only half an hour long, but it takes a whole day in the studio and involves a massive crew.

So here's our challenge. Do you know what to do to get the show live?!

Before you start - answer this question. How many people do you reckon are involved in Blue Peter? Have a guess. Write it here _____. And then compare your answer with the photo on page 110.

## AND NOW... LET'S MAKE SOME TV!

**Who knows what colour I'll end up!**

## 1

### MAKE-UP

First things first. You need us looking beautiful! As bizarre as it may sound, even boys need make-up. Without it, the hot TV studio lights can make us look shiny and show up all your spots.

## 3

### WARDROBE

Next - what to wear? We don't always know what we'll be doing, so our stylist always brings in a huge choice of outfits. Plus Helen loves clothes!!

## 2

**I'm just going to twirl this bit here, OK?**

### HAIR

And Andy, of course, well Andy needs his hair done exactly as he likes it. It's not easy to keep that famous "pineapple" hairstyle in shape.

**Be careful with the pineapple!**

**Can I wear Joel's jeans - please?!**

**So now we're ready...**

## PSSST! DON'T TELL ANYONE

**SECRET NUMBER ONE: What the studio really looks like**
This is the view you never experience on TV, complete with cameras, lights and studio producers. This is how the presenters see it. So now you know...

**5**

### MIC-UP

Nearly there... Just got to put our microphones on. They're small and black and are normally hidden on our clothes, but if you watch carefully at home, you can sometimes spot them peeping out.

**4**

### LIGHTING

In the studio, the final tweaks are being made to the set-up. We share our space with other programmes, so the hundreds of lights have to be adjusted every time. The studio is worth millions of pounds, so the pole is surprisingly lo-tech: it's used to bash the lights into position!

**What's going on here?**

**I was hoping you knew!**

Editor

# 6

## REHEARSAL

And it's time to start rehearsing! Joel is trying out a quiz with singer Ellie Goulding. Even though our script is written beforehand, things don't turn out quite how you expect. We often have to rehearse things two or three times to get them right.

# 7

## FINAL MEETING

It's not just us checking that things are OK. The editor makes notes during the rehearsals, and then everyone gets together to discuss what needs to change. By the way, things are getting a bit tight now. It's probably only fifteen minutes now till we're live on BBC One.

# PSSST! DON'T TELL ANYONE

**SECRET NUMBER TWO: A lunchtime exclusive!**
Something else we've never revealed before. At lunchtime, Helen takes Barney to the Blue Peter garden for a bit of exercise - and Joel and Andy pop down to the local market to pick up a takeaway curry. Jerk chicken, to be precise. You read it here first...

# PRODUCER

We discuss the last-minute changes with our studio producers. If there are a lot of changes, it can get a bit tense. But most times we try to relax. Anyway, that's what makes the best shows: when we're all enjoying it!

Leonie

# PETS

And here are the real stars of the show: the pets! They're relaxing at the back of the studio until they're needed on set. Lucy and Barney - they're great friends now! Amazingly, Leonie has been looking after the dogs in the studio for more than 20 years.

10

Director

# DIRECTOR

Just minutes to go. In the gallery above the studio, the director is checking all the screens, making final decisions about which cameras to use and when. The images you see at home are selected here, so everyone listens super-carefully to what the director says.

Floor Manager

11

# FLOOR MANAGER

Ten. Nine. Eight. The floor manager counts down the final ten seconds to the start of the show. After four, he stops talking, so you don't hear him on TV. He signals the final numbers with his fingers. Three. Two. One. Here we go...

12

"Hello, and welcome to Blue Peter".
We're live on air. You've done it!

# 10 THINGS YOU DIDN'T KNOW ABOUT Joel

**1** My middle name is Nermaland. Yes, honestly, my full name is Joel Nermaland Defries. But I don't even know exactly how it's spelt. It's an Indian name which my mum and dad gave me because they were really into Indian meditation and thought it was really cool. It means "egoless one", apparently.

**2** My mum and dad are called Simon and Andrea. They're ten times crazier than me. They are my toughest critics but also my highest praisers. They love it most when I make people smile.

One of my highlights: designing and modelling a T-shirt for London Fashion Week.

**3** I love making and giving people the smallest cards possible. It's just my thing. People aren't expecting to get such tiny cards, and it always makes them smile.

**4** The best present I ever got was a PlayStation 2, when I got the marks I needed in my GCSEs. I already had a PlayStation1, but the PS2 was a massive step up. I was chuffed.

**5** I love the English language, and I'd love to be really good at writing. I really admire people who can express themselves well.

**6** Something my mum always used to say to me was "pride comes before a fall". You can't be too proud about anything.

**7** If I could have anyone come to my party, I'd have Cheryl Cole, Simon Cowell, Barney the dog and Rachel Bilson from The OC.

**8** I think I'm six foot tall but in fact I'm probably five foot eleven.

**9** When I'm going on holiday the one thing I pack is tiny shorts. I just think they're fun.

**10** My biggest fans are my aunties and my granny. My auntie Anne told me recently that she has never missed an episode of Blue Peter since I started. I told her I'd never sung on Blue Peter, and she said, yes you have, and I said no I haven't, and she said, yes you have, you and Andy had a sing-off in front of JLS. And I remembered she was right.

Joel's recent challenges include rowing across the Channel, catwalk modelling and climbing Britain's tallest crane. What challenge do you think Joel should take on next?

# PERFECT PAPER PLANE

SO, YOU MAY THINK YOU KNOW HOW TO MAKE A PAPER PLANE. WRONG! WE GOT IN ONE OF BRITAIN'S TOP AERONAUTICAL EXPERTS, AND HE SHOWED US HOW TO MAKE THE ULTIMATE PAPER FLYING MACHINE. YOU WON'T REGRET IT. PROMISE.

## STAGE 1

Put your piece of A4 paper flat on a table and fold it in half lengthways.

## STAGE 2

Open the paper and fold the two top corners down the centre line that the fold has made.

## You will need:

- A piece of A4 paper
- A pen
- A pair of hands

# MAKE IT

## STAGE 3

Now fold that pointy end right over, and make a dot about two centimetres from the point.

## STAGE 4

Fold the two new corners over, so they touch this dot in the centre.

## STAGE 5

Get the small pointed end that's poking out, and fold it back over the corners.

## STAGE 6

Fold the plane down the middle again.

## STAGE 7

Put the plane on its side on the table, and make the first wing by folding along where the dotted line is in the picture.

## STAGE 8

Turn the plane over and fold the second wing. Your paper plane is now ready to fly!!

## DID YOU KNOW?

The world record for the longest paper plane flight is 27.9 seconds. See if you can beat that!

67

# WORLD TOUR

## Going Globa[l]

....................... Million

United Kingdom
62 ..... Million

....................... Million

....................... Million

....................... Million

....................... Million

....................... Million

We explored loads of countries in our mission to bring the world to your living room. But how much do you know about these far-flung shores?

Here are five of the countries we visited this year, plus their total populations (in millions of people). But of course they're jumbled up! Match them up and work out where they are on the map. To get you started, we've already done our own fair country.

BRAZIL

49m

72m

INDIA

TURKEY

192m

SOUTH AFRICA

1,182m

309m

US[A]

## Channel Challenge

Joel also travelled to another country, France - but only for about five minutes! He rowed there, turned around, and then went back again. See if you can get Joel all the way across the English Channel without bumping into ships, waves or man-eating sharks*.

START
BONNE CHANCE!

*There aren't actually man-eating sharks in the Channel - but it does make it sound more exciting...

TRÉS BIEN!

FINIS[H]

YOU MADE [IT]

# FIND YOUR PERFECT CHALLENGE!

We love nothing more than a challenge! It's our absolute ultimate favourite thing.
But if you were a Blue Peter presenter, what challenge would you most love to take on?

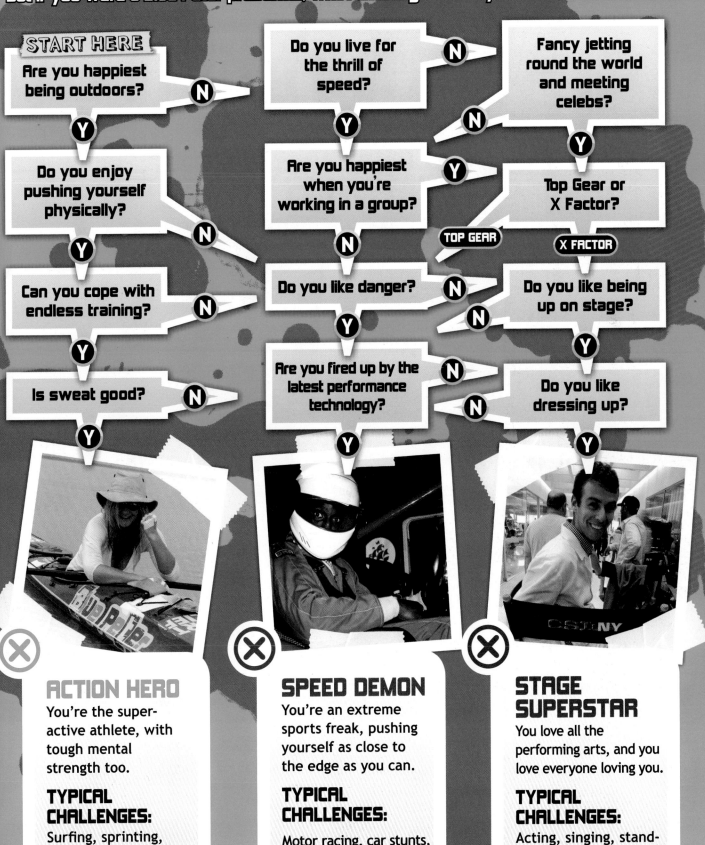

**START HERE**

Are you happiest being outdoors? **N** → 

**Y** ↓

Do you enjoy pushing yourself physically? **N** →

**Y** ↓

Can you cope with endless training? **N** →

**Y** ↓

Is sweat good? **N** →

**Y** ↓

---

Do you live for the thrill of speed? **N** →

**Y** ↓

Are you happiest when you're working in a group? **Y** →

**N** ↓

Do you like danger? **N** →

**Y** ↓

Are you fired up by the latest performance technology? **N** →

**Y** ↓

---

Fancy jetting round the world and meeting celebs? **N** →

**Y** ↓

Top Gear or X Factor?

**TOP GEAR**      **X FACTOR**

Do you like being up on stage? **N** →

**Y** ↓

Do you like dressing up? **N** →

**Y** ↓

---

## ACTION HERO
You're the super-active athlete, with tough mental strength too.

### TYPICAL CHALLENGES:
Surfing, sprinting, marathon running, rollerhockey, kayaking

**HELEN** is your closest presenter match.

## SPEED DEMON
You're an extreme sports freak, pushing yourself as close to the edge as you can.

### TYPICAL CHALLENGES:
Motor racing, car stunts, free running, skydiving, bungy jumping.

**ANDY** is your closest presenter match.

## STAGE SUPERSTAR
You love all the performing arts, and you love everyone loving you.

### TYPICAL CHALLENGES:
Acting, singing, stand-up comedy, doing impressions, dancing.

**JOEL** is your closest presenter match.

# SUPER-COOLING ICE SLUSHIE!

WE MADE THIS AT THE HEART OF WINTER, BUT IT'LL BE EVEN BETTER AT THE HEIGHT OF SUMMER. GET CREATING, GET CRUSHING - AND GET COOLING DOWN...!

## You will need:

- 1 fruit teabag
- Sugar
- Ice cubes
- Saucepan
- Blender
- Cups

## STEP 1

Make a cup of fruit tea (and take out the teabag!). Tip it into a pan over a low heat and add two cups of sugar. Stir the mixture slowly until all the sugar has dissolved into syrup and starts to bubble. Remove it from the heat.

## STEP 2

Let the syrup cool right down and pour it into a plastic container with a lid. Keep it in the fridge (it'll last for a few days). It's really important that your syrup is completely cold, so it doesn't melt the ice.

## STEP 3

Get your ice cubes and put them in a blender. Whizz them around until they look like slushy snow. You might need to add some cold water to help. (We found that doing about three cubes at a time using the small blender attachment worked well.)

## STEP 4

Put your icy slush into a cup or a glass and pour some cold syrup over the top. You'll need about the same amount of syrup as when you make squash. Cool!

## SUPER-COOL TEMPERATURE RECORDS

57.8 °C: The world's hottest temperature, recorded in 1922 in Libya in Africa.

38.5 °C: The UK's hottest temperature, recorded in 2003 in Faversham in Kent.

-27.2 °C: The UK's coldest temperature, recorded in 1895, 1982 and 1995 in Northern Scotland.

-89.2 °C: The world's coldest temperature, recorded in 1983 in Vostock in Antarctica.

# HOLLYWOOD (MIS)ADVENTURE!

## Ultimate Challenge!

HOLLYWOOD

Hollywood - here I come!

Ever since I was seven, when I first "acted" at school, I've wanted to be on stage. And so I've decided to have a go for real. I'm attempting something really big: to become a Hollywood actor. My goal in this ultimate challenge is to learn how to act, and to try to appear in a film or TV show.

**SO NOTHING BIG THEN.**

## DID YOU KNOW?

The famous sign was put up in 1923 to advertise a housing development, and originally read "HOLLYWOODLAND".

I don't know what I'm letting myself in for!

**You're kidding, right?**

Unfortunately it doesn't get off to a good start. I sign up with an amazing acting coach, Dee Cannon, who's worked with stars like Billie Piper and Bond girl Gemma Arterton.

**gry, I'm angry**

But Dee isn't impressed with my first attempt. She gives me acting lessons to improve my technique and "inner confidence". Her classes include things like acting as a chimp (!), and at times I feel a bit stupid. But Dee says that when I believe I'm being the character, I'm much more convincing. I feel like I'm progressing.

**"Hi, yes, I'm Mikey..."**

**really have to focus ou want to make it.**

**nervous!**

**Just be very open and confident in yourself.**

Next step is to have a go at something for real. The guys at Casualty very kindly let me act out a mini-scene with Charlie, Jay and Sister Bateman - and they seem to like it.

The final piece of the jigsaw is advice from some Hollywood superstars. Zac Efron tells me it will be tough, but reassures me that he still gets nervous before auditions. I act briefly with Emma Thompson, who plays Nanny McPhee, and at first she says I'm acting like a cartoon person! But a few words of wisdom from her make a complete difference.

**AND THEN I'M OUT OF TIME. THERE IS NOTHING MORE I CAN DO. THE FLIGHTS ARE BOOKED; THE BLUE PETER CAMERAS ARE READY; I AM OFF TO HOLLYWOOD TO SEE IF I CAN MAKE IT!**

## DID YOU KNOW?

The first Hollywood movie was shot here in 1911 because it was cheap and had good weather.

By the 1920s it was the centre of the US film industry and numerous film stars lived here.

Hollywood is actually part of Los Angeles

Only 120,000 people live in the district itself.

About 500 movies are made in Hollywood every year

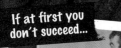

If at first you don't succeed...

...try, try again...

Hollywood in California. Tinseltown. The city of dreams. The most famous movie-making place on earth. The place where budding actors and actresses head every year to try to make their fortune. But for every person who makes it as a star, there are thousands more who don't – who end up working as waiters and waitresses.

**Have you auditioned before?**

**This is my third time - I drove 30 hours to be here today.**

And now one more wannabe has joined their ranks. A certain J Defries. With all of three months' acting experience.

I've only got two weeks here, but I'm going to make the most of it. So I go and see agent after agent - they're the people who can help you see casting directors for movies. I even do some auditions. But after the first week, nothing is coming my way. I think my acting has improved, but it's not improved enough.

**Amazing! I just don't think I've got his passion!**

A bit depressed, I go to visit one of our friends, Miley Cyrus, on the set of Hannah Montana. She tells me that often auditions are nothing about you at all - it's just that sometimes they have an idea in their head of what they want, and it's not you. Her advice cheers me up.

It's not that you're doing it bad, Joel, it's just that you might not be what they're looking for.

THEN, WITH A FEW DAYS LEFT, I STRIKE LUCKY AND GET A PART AS AN EXTRA IN LEGENDARY US TV COP SHOW CSI: NEW YORK. AN EXTRA IS A PERSON WHO'S IN THE BACK OF THE PICTURE WHILE THE MAIN ACTOR IS TALKING. THOUGH YOU DON'T GET TO SAY ANYTHING, LOTS OF PEOPLE WANT TO BE EXTRAS, BECAUSE IT GETS YOU CLOSER TO THE REAL THING.

But I'm surprised to find that I don't enjoy it. I hang around all day, just to do the same walk five times over. Everyone here seems to be hanging around wanting to be famous - and it strikes me that that's not much of a life.

In my last few days I call a few more agents and do a couple more auditions, but my heart's no longer in it. Hollywood is a crazy place. This hasn't been a negative experience at all. But I've realised that it can take you 10 or 20 years out here, just hoping and wondering, and even then you'll probably not make it. That's not a life for me.

CSI:NY

I got - briefly - on TV, but what I've really understood is that my childhood dream isn't realistic. I like my life as it is. I don't need to chase another dream. In that sense, although maybe I didn't really achieve my challenge, it's been a total success.

**START**

**Have you got what it takes?!**

When I kayaked down the Amazon, it wasn't just my tiredness I had to fight. There were a whole load of risks which could slow me down - or at worst end my challenge altogether. Your mission: see how quickly you can battle past my top ten risks and get to the finish line.

## HELEN'S VARIATION !

If your two dice match the exact numbers (eg 1 and 6 for Lightning), miss out the next risk and jump to the one after that.

### 1. LIGHTNING

There were constant storms, and if it gets you, lighting can kill you. But we took shelter fast, so there wasn't much chance of that!

| HOW LIKELY?: 1 | DANGER FACTOR: 7 |
| HOW SEVERE?: 6 | ROLLS: ☐ ☐ ☐ |

### 2. CAPSIZING

Kayaks are tiny compared to the massive Amazon. But they're built to float, so if I rolled over I was pretty sure I could get out OK.

| HOW LIKELY?: 3 |
| HOW SEVERE?: 2 |
| DANGER FACTOR: 5 |
| ROLLS: ☐ ☐ ☐ |

### 5. SUNSTROKE

I actually got heat exhaustion, and the searing temperatures meant I had to take this very seriously. Recovery times are fast, though.

| HOW LIKELY?: 6 |
| HOW SEVERE?: 2 |
| DANGER FACTOR: 8 |
| ROLLS: ☐ ☐ ☐ |

### 3. ALLIGATOR

We saw a few of these hunting at the river bank. I wouldn't like to meet one so we steered well clear!

| HOW LIKELY?: 2 |
| HOW SEVERE?: 6 |
| DANGER FACTOR: 8 |
| ROLLS: ☐ ☐ ☐ |

### 4. ACCIDENT

It was slippery and choppy, so there was always a risk I could bash or gash myself somewhere. But I'm confident I could have continued.

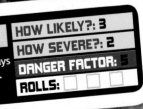

| HOW LIKELY?: 3 |
| HOW SEVERE?: 2 |
| DANGER FACTOR: 5 |
| ROLLS: ☐ ☐ ☐ |

# RAINFOREST
## SURVIVAL MISSION

**CAN YOU GET DOWN THE AMAZON AND SURVIVE ALL THE DANGERS ALONG THE WAY?**

### HOW TO PLAY

Get two dice. For each risk, shake the exact danger factor before going to the next stage. Write down how many rolls of the dice it took, and add them up at the end. We've added space for three missions, or to play against two friends.

### 10. SICKNESS

The top risk. Impure water, germs in food, insect bites - on expeditions like this they hit the crew at any time. Can be anything from a day of diahorrhea or potentially life-threatening.

| | |
|---|---|
| HOW LIKELY?: 5 | DANGER FACTOR: 11 |
| HOW SEVERE?: 6 | ROLLS: ☐ ☐ ☐ |

**FINISH**

**You made it! Well done!** Now total up how long it took you to get here!

### HOW DID YOU RATE?

**10-20 ROLLS**
Wow! You're speedy - fancy joining me on my next challenge?!

**20-40 ROLLS**
Not bad - just need to navigate those risks a bit faster next time.

**40 OR MORE**
Uh-oh - you attract trouble! I'm steering well clear! Try again...

**TOTAL SCORES:** ☐ ☐ ☐

### 6. PIRANHAS

There was a lot of talk about these supposedly flesh-eating fish, but most experts said they weren't really a threat and wouldn't really eat you. Overrated.

| | |
|---|---|
| HOW LIKELY?: 1 | |
| HOW SEVERE?: 3 | |
| DANGER FACTOR: 4 | |
| ROLLS: ☐ ☐ ☐ | |

### 9. RIVER COLLISION

With boats, tankers and hidden tree trunks right along the river, I had to keep my eyes peeled the whole time, and the speed of the water made them harder to avoid than you might think.

| | |
|---|---|
| HOW LIKELY?: 4 | |
| HOW SEVERE?: 5 | |
| DANGER FACTOR: 9 | |
| ROLLS: ☐ ☐ ☐ | |

### 8. COFFEE BURN

A surprisingly common "injury" on BBC filming trips - but given the fact that I don't like coffee, I'd be amazed if it got me!

| | |
|---|---|
| HOW LIKELY?: 1 | |
| HOW SEVERE?: 1 | |
| DANGER FACTOR: 2 | |
| ROLLS: ☐ ☐ ☐ | |

### 7. CAR CRASH

On all foreign filming trips, this is actually often the number one risk. You have to take taxis everywhere, and people drive like maniacs. Very ordinary, but lethal.

| | |
|---|---|
| HOW LIKELY?: 4 | |
| HOW SEVERE?: 6 | |
| DANGER FACTOR: 10 | |
| ROLLS: ☐ ☐ ☐ | |

## WHO WILL WIN WHEN WE EACH CUSTOMISE AN INDIAN RICKSHAW?

During our trip to India, we often took rides in rickshaws: little motorised taxis you can hop in and out of. So we came up with the idea of giving them a Blue Peter-style makeover. But the twist was that each of us would do one in our own sweet way. Who would create the one with the most style and customer satisfaction? THE BATTLE WAS ON!

Helen wanted hers to be bright and colourful and comfortable. So she sprayed it white and painted Indian henna-style patterns on the outside. On the inside, she layered it with soft fabrics, silks and comfy cushions. Definitely one for the girls.

And Joel. Oh Joel. He can't drive, so for a start he only got a rickety cycle rickshaw. And he turned it into a mobile version of the most famous building in India, the Taj Mahal, complete with Taj Mahal helmet and drainpipes painted white for the minarets.

Andy loves his music, so called his the "Bhangrashaw", after Indian bhangra music. He painted big bold dancing figures on the outside, and inside installed a glitter ball, neon lighting and a music system! The glammest rickshaw Mumbai has ever seen.

Then it was time to hit the streets. As predicted, Helen picked up loads of very happy girls. Andy wowed his customers with the coolest rickshaw experience around. And Joel – well he struggled to get many passengers at all, but when he finally gave a ride to two children, they said it was an experience they'd remember all their lives!

SO WHO WON? As judge, we had Andrew, an international style and bling guru from Mumbai. And for him, in terms of boldness and inventiveness, there was only one winner. J-O-E-L.

# WELL DONE, YOU CRAZY DUDE!

# BADGE

# BRAINBOX!

The Blue Peter badge is one of the most highly sought-after prizes in British television. But how do you get one? The six types of badge are pictured below. See if you can work out from the descriptions which badge is which!

This badge is very rare and only awarded for really outstanding achievements, such as saving someone's life or doing something truly extraordinary that benefits other people.

**BADGE COLOUR:**

If you write or email us with something different from what you won your Blue badge for, then you're in with a chance of winning this badge!

**BADGE COLOUR:**

You can win this badge for telling us about something you're doing that's helping the environment, or for letters and pictures about conservation or nature.

**BADGE COLOUR:**

Winners and runners up of Blue Peter competitions get this badge. To win one of these badges you have to enter a Blue Peter competition (obviously!).

**BADGE COLOUR:**

Review an episode of Blue Peter by filling in the form which you can print out from the Blue Peter website. If you do that, you could win this colour badge.

**BADGE COLOUR:**

This badge is awarded for interesting letters or emails, poems, pictures, really good ideas for the programme, pictures and for having appeared on the programme.

**BADGE COLOUR:**

## DID YOU KNOW?

- You need to be aged between 6 and 15 to get a badge

- You will also get a Badge Card, which means you can get in free to 200 places around the UK

- Top attractions include Alton Towers, the Eden Project and Sealife Centres.

ANSWERS ON PAGE 110.

← Silver badge

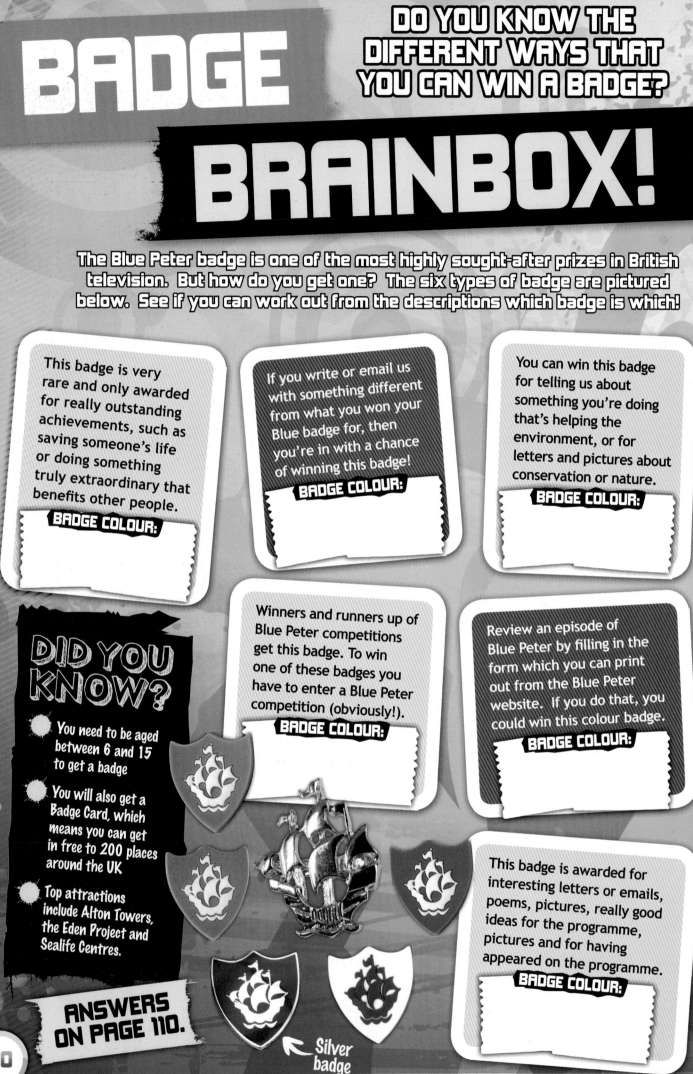

# QUICK CHALLENGE

# CHRISTMAS WINDOWS

1. Andy and I decided we'd find out all we could about the cut-throat, billion-pound world of Christmas shopping by having a go at making our own Christmas window displays.

2. We each had one window to decorate, to see which one would draw more people into the store at this crucial time of year.

3. A good window display can make thousands of pounds of difference to a shop. If it gets you in the store, it's done its job very well. If you walk on by, it's failed.

**We can see your pants, you know**

JOEL

4. We worked hard all day, with only a short break to dress up as a pantomime horse and walk around the department store while being filmed by our camera crew. As you do.

**Vote for me!**

ANI

5. So to our final window displays. Andy went for modern and funky with bright but unusual colours, whereas I...

6. I went for a traditional approach, all tinsel, trees and fake snow. And who won? We got children to vote for their favourite, and there was one clear winner.

**No, vote for ME!**

It was Andy. Boo hiss.

# CELEB GUEST:
# THE MIZ

## TOP STATS

**Full name:** Michael Mizanin
**Job:** Professional wrestler
**Main home:** Los Angeles, USA

## QUICKFIRE QUESTIONS

**How do you do such great trash talk before a fight?**

"Here's what you gotta do: you've got to be entertaining and have a great, great finish. So if I was to trash talk right now, I would say: 'Right now on Blue Peter, you have the United States champion, the most charismatic and entertaining superstar in WWE. I have more gold than Mr T. I am the reason people are watching Blue Peter right now! You know why? Cos I'm the Miz!'"

**Have you got any advice for Blue Peter viewers?**

"I'd say: I can do anything I put my mind to, just as you kids can put your mind to anything, and do it all!"

## TRUE OR FALSE?

1. The Miz was studying business at university when he quit to join a reality TV show.

☐ TRUE ☐ FALSE

2. Despite his tough image, he is a big animal lover, and has four dogs, seven cats and a pet racoon.

☐ TRUE ☐ FALSE

3. The Miz holds the world record for the greatest number of one-armed press-ups in one hour: 2,467.

☐ TRUE ☐ FALSE

## KEY DATES

**8 October 1980:** Born in Ohio, USA. **2001:** Stars in the first of several reality TV shows, MTV's The Real World **1 September 2006:** Makes his WWE TV wrestling debut, winning against Tatanka. **5 October 2009:** Crowned WWE United States Champion for the first time.

ANSWERS: Only 1 is true. 2 and 3 are completely made up, sorry.

TOP STATS
Full name:
Jahmaal Noel Fyffe
Job: Rapper
Main home:
London, UK

# CELEB GUEST:
# CHIPMUNK

## QUICKFIRE QUESTIONS

**Who inspires you to sing?**

"I wouldn't say there was one person directly. I used to be in my local youth club, where if you never had a lyric, you weren't really cool. So you start with the words and go from there. I was pretty rubbish, but time went by and we just practised with the vinyl, and I just mastered my craft from there and made a name for myself."

**Were you good as a rapper when you were young?**

"I wasn't really fluent 'til I was about fourteen. For me it's like anything you believe in: if you put the work in, you'll make it."

## TRUE OR FALSE?

**1.** A friend gave him the nickname Chipmunk because of the way his teeth look.

☐ TRUE ☐ FALSE

**2.** He says that he might change his name so that he's known as Mr Chip.

☐ TRUE ☐ FALSE

**3.** Oopsy Daisy - with Dayo Olatunji - was his second number one single.

☐ TRUE ☐ FALSE

## KEY DATES

**26 November 1990:** Born in London, UK. **16 January 2009:** First single, Chip Diddy Chip, is released and reaches number 25. **30 September 2009:** Wins Best Hip-Hop Act at the MOBO black music awards. **12 October 2009:** Releases debut album, I Am Chipmunk, going on to sell 300,000 copies.

Chip recreates his first kiss...

ANSWERS: 1 is true; 2 and 3 are false. He says he might change his name to Mr Munk; and Oopsy Daisy was in fact his first number one single.

83

# WEIRDEST SIGHTS RATED

CHECK OUT SOME OF THE ODDEST-LOOKING
DISCOVERIES WE MADE OVER THE PAST YEAR.

## 3D ART

**What is it?** A flat floor painting that looks like it's in 3D

| IMPRESSIVE: 7 | WEIRD: 2 |
|---|---|
| COOL: 6 | PRICE: 3 |

**How it works:** It's all about what artists call the "vanishing point". If you draw something stretched out on the floor, and look at it in a certain way, it looks like it's standing up.

**Did you know:** Your natural 3D vision isn't actually complete until you're about six, when your nerves, muscles and brain cells are fully formed and working together.

*You can see how this painting really looks in the photo on page 61!*

## BIG MAN

**What is it?** An 8-metre-high blue man, who's been walking across Scotland.

| IMPRESSIVE: 8 | WEIRD: 4 |
|---|---|
| COOL: 7 | PRICE: 10 |

**How it works:** It's actually a massive puppet, weighing 1.5 tonnes and held up by a forklift truck. Joel joined the team of 12 puppeteers, who operate it as it walks along.

**Did you know?** Big Man is the UK's biggest puppet, but the world's biggest puppet, built in the USA in 2007, was an incredible 15 metres tall.

## GIANT PIANO

**What is it?** The UK's largest piano - stretching up to 7.5 metres long

| IMPRESSIVE: 6 | WEIRD: 5 |
|---|---|
| COOL: 4 | PRICE: 6 |

**How it works:** A bit like a massive Dance Mat, this huge one-off floor piano has special software telling you when to play which key.

**Did you know?** Most pianos have 88 keys: 36 black keys and 52 white keys. Our giant piano had only 60 keys - but it was about ten times as big!

# TOAST ART

**What is it?** Portraits painted in Marmite on toast

| IMPRESSIVE: 9 | WEIRD: 6 |
|---|---|
| COOL: 10 | PRICE: 1 |

**How it works:** You're artist Nathan Wyburn from Wales. You see a picture of Simon Cowell. You get some Marmite and paint it on 30 pieces of toast. Um, that's it.

**Did you know?** Simon Cowell loves cars and has a Ferrari, Bentley, Mini Cooper and Rolls Royce Phantom. Does he love toast? We've got no idea!

# EXPLODING PUMPKINS

**What is it?** Chemical foam that bursts out of a pumpkin

| IMPRESSIVE: 5 | WEIRD: 4 |
|---|---|
| COOL: 7 | PRICE: 2 |

**How it works:** Inside a pumpkin, mix soap with two chemicals: hydrogen peroxide and *Sorry – deleted for safety reasons* Stand well back. Within seconds, the chemical reaction causes foam to explode out.

**Did you know?** Giant pumpkins are grown from specially-bred seeds. The biggest pumpkin ever was grown in 2009 and weighed 782kg –that's as heavy as a small car.

# EXPLODING WATER BOTTLE

**What is it?** Blowing up a hot water bottle until it bursts

| IMPRESSIVE: 6 | WEIRD: 10 |
|---|---|
| COOL: 1 | PRICE: 1 |

**How it works:** Crazy strongman Shaun Jones loves setting world records. He took just 18.81 seconds on Blue Peter to blow up a hot water bottle until it burst. Why? Who knows?!

**Did you know?** Eduard Penkala from Croatia invented the hot water bottle about 100 years ago. He also invented a rail-car brake and an anode battery. Why? Who knows?! (x2)

# GRUESOME GREAT BRITAIN

WE LIFT THE LID ON THE UK'S GRUESOME PAST -
AND DISCOVER THE GORY JOBS KIDS USED TO DO

## VIKINGS

Vikings used wee to bleach their hair.

Yeuch!

## WHEN:

793-1066

## WHO:

Raiders from Scandinavia who attacked and settled in parts of the UK

## VIKING SLAVE CHILD

When the Vikings raided villages, they made 'native' Anglo-Saxon children do all the horrible jobs that no-one else wanted to. Jobs included mucking out pigs, gutting fish and grinding corn. Yikes!

Andy got lessons in how to be a fearsome Viking raider. He discovered that Vikings gave their swords names, such as Leg Biter or Fast Cutter. So Andy called his... Tallulah.

FLOYD AND CONNOR'S GROSS RATING:
## 4 OUT OF 5

# MEDIEVAL

Us knights are brave and fearless in battle!

Humph!

Don't forget chivalry: you need to be thoughtful and generous too.

## KIDS' JOB
## BARBER-SURGEON'S ASSISTANT

Barber-surgeons were cheap doctors. As well as cutting your hair, they would fix illnesses and cut off limbs. The assistant's jobs included squeezing boils, cleaning teeth and mopping up blood. Yuk!

Andy and Joel attacked the castle using a trebuchet – a catapult that flung everything from rocks (to smash the walls) to diseased bodies (to spread infection among inhabitants.

Corey's gross rating:
## 4 out of 5

87

# Tudors

At one banquet here, Henry VIII served 2,000 sheep...

...and a roasted dolphin!

## Kids' job

## Tudor servant boys

It was a time of great excess, and rich people needed lots of servants. Jobs for children included plucking pigeons, blowing up sheep bladders to make footballs and cleaning poo out of toilet holes. Yum!

Helen and Joel made violin strings Tudor-style, by twirling spaghetti-like strips of catgut together. Catgut is in fact made of sliced sheep's intestines. Yum.

*Floyd and Connor's gross rating:*
## 5 out of 5

# VICTORIANS

**Victorian men were never seen outside without a hat.**

**My turn!**

**WHEN:**
1837-1901

**WHAT:**
A time of prosperity and poverty under one monarch, Queen Victoria

J. WILTSH

CHOCOLATE

## KIDS JOB

# COTTON MILL WORKERS

Victorian industry required a huge number of workers, and poor children as young as eight did everything from threading cotton onto machines to cleaning the machines when they were running. Yow!

Joel saw millions of maggots being bred at a maggot farm. The Victorians realised that maggots gave off ammonia which helped stop killer disease TB, so they slept with trays of them under their beds.

JAE-LEANNE AND MIA'S GROSS RATING:
**3 OUT OF 5**

For Mabel's last programme, we were joined by Katy Hill, who was the Blue Peter presenter who first brought Mabel to the show. Hundreds of you also sent in goodbye and good luck cards for Mabel, which we used to decorate the whole studio. Thank you!

# 10 THINGS YOU DIDN'T KNOW ABOUT

# The pets

**1** Mabel retired from Blue Peter this year: a sad day for us, but for Mabel it was the right thing, since she was getting more and more elderly and was finding it more difficult to cope with the studio. Mabel had been on Blue Peter for over 14 years, having joined us on 19 February 1996.

**2** The story of how Mabel joined the show is really quite special. Katy Hill, one of the presenters back then, made a report in January 1996 about dogs who had been rescued by the RPSCA. During the filming, she met a Border Collie cross at the rehoming centre. The whole team fell in love with her, so one month later, Mabel drove into Studio 1 at Television Centre with RSPCA Inspector Mark Buggie and joined the team.

**3** Mabel got her name from Mark's initials on the kennel she was kept in: M. A. B. 1.

**4** During her career, Mabel starred alongside 14 Blue Peter presenters.

The pets love any excuse to dress up! Here is Mabel dressed up for Halloween.

**5** Lucy is the sixth dog to have joined Blue Peter. She joined just three years after Mabel, in 1999. Lucy is a pedigree Golden Retriever.

**6** Socks joined the show on 4 January 2006, and was the first ragdoll cat on Blue Peter. We chose ragdolls because they're a breed which like indoor life, making them perfect for the studio.

**7** Cookie is younger than Socks, but bizarrely he is Sock's uncle.

**8** Shelley is Blue Peter's fifth tortoise, following Freda, Maggie, Jim and George. Shelley is a Mediterranean spur-thigh tortoise, like George - who died aged about 80 after 22 years on the show. George is also the only pet to be buried in the Blue Peter garden.

**9** Barney is Blue Peter's ninth official dog, following Petra, Patch, Shep, Goldie, Bonnie, Mabel, Lucy and Meg (former presenter Matt Baker's dog). Barney belongs to and lives with Helen.

**10** Years ago, Blue Peter also had parrots as pets. Bizarrely, the second parrot was also called Barney.

Barney has been on various filming trips with Helen, including when she had singing lessons, took part in a medieval tournament and cleaned up the Blue Peter garden. What type of filming trip would you like him to go on next?!

# BRILLIANT BADGES

CUSTOMISE YOUR CLOTHES OR BAGS WITH THIS EASY-TO-MAKE BADGE DESIGN. YOU COULD MAKE SOMETHING GROOVY, LIKE THIS STRAWBERRY ON MY DENIM JACKET. OR CREATE A SIMPLE NAME TAG, WHICH YOU COULD USE IN HUNDREDS OF PLACES!

## You will need:
- Felt ● Badge or safety pin
- Needle and thread
- Fabric glue ● Cotton wool
- Sequins or gems for decoration

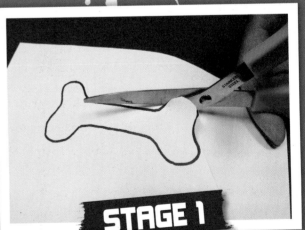

## STAGE 1

Draw your design on to a piece of paper and cut it out with scissors.

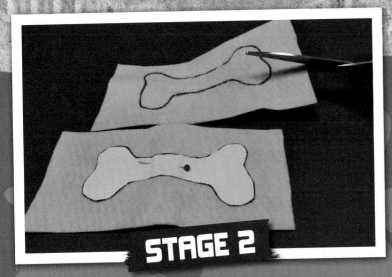

## STAGE 2

Draw around your template using a felt-tip pen (you could pin it to the felt to stop it moving). Do this twice, so you've got both the front and the back pieces. Cut both pieces out.

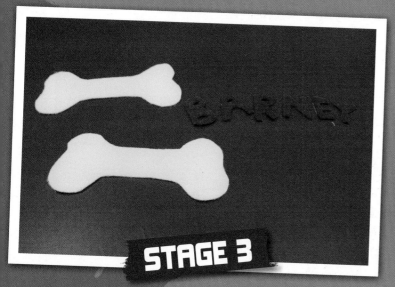

## STAGE 3

If you want, you can now decorate the front piece of felt. Use sequins, gems, felt letters, or anything that will funk it up. Stick your decorations on with fabric glue.

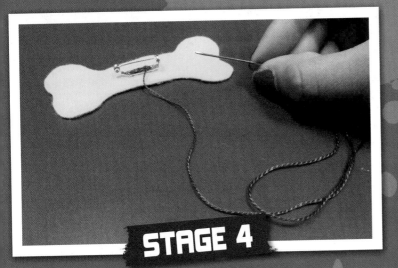

## STAGE 4

Sew your safety pin to the back of the badge (you might want an adult to help with the sewing).

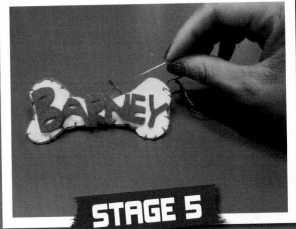

## STAGE 5

Now sew the front and back pieces together. Blanket stitch is best - if you don't know how to do this, there's a an easy guide on the Blue Peter website. Pause the sewing before you get all way round so there's a gap for the next step.

## STAGE 6

Use cotton wool to stuff your badge through the gap. Then continue sewing until you've got all the way round and tie off. And now your badge is finished. Awesome! Why not have a go at another one?

# Blue Peter MEGA QUIZ

We love making Blue Peter - but we hope you like watching it too. So we've come up with a whole load of questions about the past year on Blue Peter, graded according to difficulty. Hopefully you'll know the first five - but for the last five, well, even we might struggle!

## EASY

**1**
Who are the presenters of Blue Peter?*
**A.** Andy, Helen, Joel
**B.** Sam, Mark, Sonali
**C.** Ethel, Stanley, Hilda

**2**
What's the name of our new pet?
**A.** Bernard
**B.** Bieber
**C.** Barney

**3**
Which river did Helen kayak down for Sport Relief?
**A.** Humber
**B.** Amazon
**C.** Nile

**4**
If you saved someone's life, what colour Blue Peter badge could you get?
**A.** Blue
**B.** Green
**C.** Gold

**5**
What bedroom item did we topple to break an unusual domino-style world record?
**A.** Mattresses
**B.** Bookshelves
**C.** Giant hairdryers

Score: /5
Hopefully you'r doing OK so far...?

94

* (We thought we'd start gentle, but this is ridiculous!)

# MEDIUM

**6** When he was learning to act, which BBC drama did Joel get to try a scene in?
A. Casualty
B. EastEnders
C. Lark Rise to Candleford

**7** How many years was Mabel a Blue Peter pet?
A. 13
B. 14
C. 15

**8** Which of these singers or bands haven't we had on the show this year?
A. JLS
B. Justin Bieber
C. Lady GaGa

**9** Which famous tower did Joel help to restore by stripping its paint?
A. Blackpool Tower
B. Eiffel Tower
C. BT Tower

**10** Which celeb won our 2010 CBBC Star Striker competition?
A. Joel Defries
B. Mark Rhodes
C. Faryl Smith

Score: /10
Perhaps we're beginning to test you...?

# HARD

**11** What birth disorder did we raise money to fix in our Send a Smile appeal?
A. Cleft lip
B. Short sight
C. Heart defects

**12** Andy and Joel battled it out in sledging, ice karting, snow running and curling for our Winter Rivals competition, but what was the fifth sport they competed in?
A. Brushball
B. Sweeperball
C. Broomball

**13** We checked out a Formula 3 racing car that's powered by something special, but what was it?
A. Peanut butter
B. Lemonade
C. Chocolate

**14** In our web game Turkish Bizarre, what do you have to collect to earn points?
A. Turkish delight
B. Caramel chews
C. Pear drops

**15** Andy mentored a team of British young people who played in the Street Child World Cup, but which city did they come from?
A. London
B. Glasgow
C. Manchester

Score: /15
Hopefully that was a bit of a challenge!

Turn to page 110 for the answers

# QUICK CHRISTMAS
## SNOWMAN SWEETS

### You will need:

- 80g margarine or butter
- White marshmallows
- Cocktail sticks
- Chocolate sticks
- Red liquorice strings or shoelaces
- Large and small chocolate buttons
- Orange dried fruit
- An edible icing pen
- Melted milk chocolate

### STEP 1

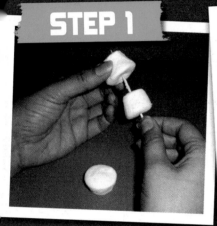

Get three white marshmallows and push them onto a cocktail stick.

### STEP 2

Give your snowman arms by sticking two bits of chocolate stick into the middle marshmallow. Then wrap your red liquorice around the bottom of the top marshmallow to make his scarf.

### STEP 3

Using the edible icing, decorate your snowman's face to give him eyes and buttons.

### STEP 4

Create his hat by using some melted chocolate to stick a small chocolate sweet on to a larger chocolate button, and then sticking that onto his head. Complete his face by sticking on a piece of dried orange fruit as his nose.

I just wanna eat them!

# TREATS
## CHOCOLATE REINDEERS

### STEP 1

Melt some milk chocolate (you might want an adult to help) and wait for it to cool down slightly. Spread some on the top of each of the tea cakes to make your reindeer's face.

## You will need:

- Chocolate tea cakes
- Raisins
- A red sweet
- Curly chocolate
- Melted milk chocolate

### STEP 2

Now get your raisins, and push them into the melted chocolate to make the eyes. Do the same with a red sweet for the nose.

### STEP 3

Then give your reindeer some antlers by sticking the cut-up pieces of curly chocolate to the top of the teacake. Put it in the fridge to set, and hey presto, it's done!

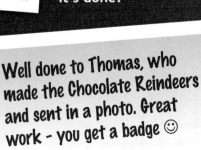

Well done to Thomas, who made the Chocolate Reindeers and sent in a photo. Great work - you get a badge ☺

# YOU SENT A SMILE

How you changed the lives of nearly 2,000 children!

## THE SATURDAYS JOINED US TO SUPPORT ONE OF THE MOST POWERFUL APPEALS WE'VE EVER ORGANISED.

Our aim was to help some of the thousands of children around the world who suffer with cleft lips and palettes. This is a defect that can occur during pregnancy when parts of the baby's mouth don't join together properly.

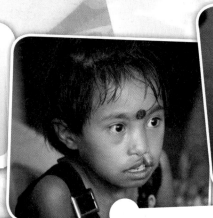

In the UK, all cleft lips and palettes are easily fixed soon after birth. But, as we found out when we visited Northern India, other countries often haven't got the money or expertise to treat everyone.

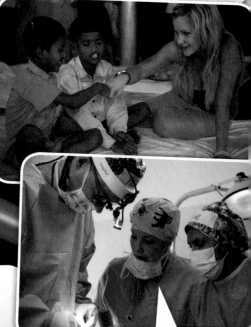

Children with clefts can have problems eating, hearing and talking, and are often bullied. Amazingly, the operation to fix it takes only 45 minutes and costs £150. That's where our appeal came in.

**I never knew it could be fixed so easily!**

# KIRAN'S STORY

I met Kiran on my first visit to India. She was a beautiful girl, but her whole life was dominated by her cleft lip and palette. It made her quiet and shy, and she was desperate to get it fixed.

Kiran was over the moon when she got selected for the 45-minute operation! She is 9, and no child in Britain would ever get to her age without having a cleft fixed.

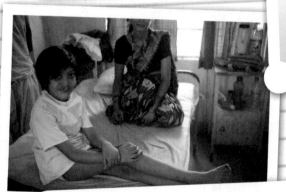

The operation was a complete success! It took Kiran a while to come back to normal, and her lip was still healing up. But over time the scar would fade.

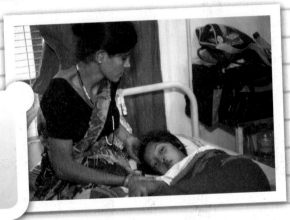

We teamed up with charity Operation Smile to give you the chance to help hundreds of these children in India get their smile back.

What we asked was incredibly simple. Every time a child has an operation to fix their cleft lip or palette, they have to wear a surgical gown. So we asked you to use your creativity and turn T-shirts into gowns.

Every gown you sent Operation Smile saved them £3. Every 50 gowns saved them £150 – enough to give another child this life-changing surgery. Children like Kiran...

And here she is six months later. What a change! Her lip looks absolutely perfect, and Kiran is happier, healthier and more confident. All thanks to one quick and cheap operation.

Blue Peter

send a smile

Operation Smile
Changing Lives One Smile at a Time

99

# YOU SENT A SMILE

The studio was buzzing with excitement when we launched the Send a Smile appeal! Every nook and cranny was packed with children and artists, all designing T-shirts as colourfully as possible.

We set a target of 20,000 gowns. But we were blown away by the response! Within days, you were sending in photos of gowns you'd designed, and whole classes got involved too.

**Lulu and Milly**

**Caitlin and Toby**

## LOADS OF CELEBS MADE GOWNS TOO

**from JLS...**

**...to Alesha Dixon...**

**...to Peter Andre**

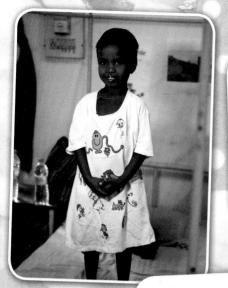

In just a few months, we got so many gowns that we smashed our original target of 20,000. In total, you sent in an amazing 92,000 gowns! That's enough to provide operations for over 1,800 children.

We went back to India with some of the gowns you'd made, and it was so moving to see all the children wearing them before their operations. In fact, you made so many gowns that Operation Smile will be able to use them for years to come.

92,000

Once again, Blue Peter viewers wowed and surprised us with your generosity and enthusiasm. You will change the lives of over 1,800 children. All that's left to say is:

Well done you guys!

This is amazing!

# THANK YOU!

# CELEB GUEST:
# RYAN GIGGS

## TOP STATS
Full name: Ryan Joseph Giggs
Job: Professional footballer
Main home: Worsley in Manchester

## QUICKFIRE QUESTIONS

*(When he won BBC Sports Personality of the Year, 2009)*

**How do you manage to sustain such fine form?**
"A mixture of things really: desire, looking after myself, enjoying it. I'm enjoying my football more than ever and that's reflected in my play."

**Do you think you're more appreciated as you get older?**
"It's unusual, at the age of 36, to be playing for a team like Manchester United for 20 years, and long may it continue!"

## TRUE OR FALSE?

**1.** Ryan's original surname was Wilson, but he started using his mum's surname, Giggs, when he was 16.
☐ **TRUE** ☐ **FALSE**

**2.** Before he signed to Manchester United, he actually joined arch-rivals Manchester City's School of Excellence.
☐ **TRUE** ☐ **FALSE**

**3.** He's the only player to score in every season of the Premier League since it started in 1992.
☐ **TRUE** ☐ **FALSE**

## KEY DATES

**29 November 1973:** Born in Cardiff in Wales. **29 November 1987:** Signs for Manchester United as a schoolboy on his 14th birthday. **12 April 1992:** Wins his first Winner's Medal, for the League Cup (now the Carling Cup) **16 May 2009:** Wins the Premier League with Manchester United for a record 11th time.

ANSWERS: They're all true!

## TOP STATS

Full name:
Emma Thompson
Job: Actress and writer
Main home:
London, UK

# CELEB GUEST:

# EMMA THOMPSON

## QUICKFIRE QUESTIONS

**What inspired you to write Nanny McPhee?**

"There are books called Nurse Matilda by Christianna Brand about this very ugly nanny who gets prettier as the story goes on. But there isn't much in those books of the story, so I've had to write this film as a completely new story."

**How long does it take to put on your make-up, and what does it feel like?**

"It only takes an hour and 15 minutes. It doesn't take me very long to look like that, so that's a little bit sad! After 10 hours you're happy getting it off."

## TRUE OR FALSE?

1. Emma originally wanted to play Hermione in the Harry Potter movies, but was told she is too old.

☐ TRUE ☐ FALSE

2. She has won two Oscars, and keeps them both in her downstairs toilet.

☐ TRUE ☐ FALSE

3. Emma still lives in the same street where she grew up in North London.

☐ TRUE ☐ FALSE

## KEY DATES

**15 April 1959:** Born in London, UK. **29 March 1993:** Wins her first Oscar, for acting in the movie Howard's End. **31 May 2004:** Stars as Professor Trelawney in Harry Potter and the Prisoner of Azkaban. **21 October 2005:** Stars as Nanny McPhee in the first of two Nanny McPhee movies, which she also wrote.

46a          47          47a

46a          47          47a

ANSWERS: 2 and 3 are true; 1 is completely made up.

103

# ULTIMATE ADVENTURE!
# FROM EUROPE TO ASIA

## ONE THOUSAND MILES ACROSS TURKEY, ON THE BEST ROAD TRIP OF OUR LIVES!

This has got to be the funkiest yellow camper van you've ever seen! It's actually a camper van with a VW Beetle welded into the roof. The perfect vehicle to explore one of Europe's least-known countries: Turkey. In fact, what's amazing about Turkey is that the far left (OK, far west for you geography experts!) is in Europe, but across the Bosphorous at Istanbul, the rest of it is in Asia.

## FIRST STOP

Oil wrestling is Turkey's craziest and most famous sport. Wrestlers grease themselves up and compete to see who can get the other one on the ground the first. The Kirkpinar tournament at Edirne has been taking place for an incredible 647 years, making it the world's longest-running sporting competition.

So, of course, Joel and Andy had to have a go! In fact, they were the first non-Turkish wrestlers ever to compete at Kirkpinar. And all those who think that Joel's skinny chest would make it harder for Andy to grip on to - well, you'd be wrong. Andy won hands down.

For safety, Helen had to shave off Joel's underarm hair!

Victory is mine!

BLACK SEA

EDIRNE
ISTANBUL
ISHAK PASHA
TURKEY
CAPPADOCIA

MEDITERRANEAN
SEA

## TO ISTANBUL!

Istanbul may be Turkey's biggest and most famous city, but in fact it's not the capital: that honour belongs to Ankara. But it does have Hagia Sophia, the building you can see on the skyline, which is famous for its massive dome.

But enough about buildings - let's do something! We all got stuck into making Turkish Delight, the country's most famous sweet. We came up with various new flavours, and bizarrely Joel's strawberries and cream flavour won the day.

Andy proved a whizz at being a whirling dervish. This spinning dance is something which a group of holy people called Sufis do in order to focus on God and get closer to perfection. Andy was surprisingly good at it. Joel just felt ill.

**Wheeeeeeee!)**

We also climbed to the top of Hagia Sophia. This legendary building was constructed in 537, and was for 1,000 years the world's biggest cathedral. It's now a museum. We then visited an amazing archaeological dig at Çatalhöyük (see page 32) before heading to...

(see page 32)

**Wheeeeeeee!**

**Andy, will you stop it now?!**

## CRAZY CAPPADOCIA

The "land of the fairy chimneys"! And you can see why it's called that. We took an early-morning hot-air balloon ride to discover more about this incredible geological formation. The chimneys were formed thousands of years ago, as wind and water eroded soft ash in the ground, leaving tougher pillars of volcanic rock behind.

But the fairy chimneys aren't just pretty to look at. The local people have also turned them into houses! Andy met one of the families who still live in these peculiar homes. And it's not just above ground that's unusual...

Over a thousand years ago, people built extraordinary underground cities where they could hide from attack. It's thought that 20,000 people could spend up to two months hiding in tunnels 10-floors deep.

**It's the worst vase I've ever seen!**

Fortunately, Joel brought us down to earth by trying out the local crafts. The area is famed for its beautiful pottery. So it's a good job, then, that Joel was only passing through...

# GOING FURTHER AND FURTHER EAST

Uh-oh, what's Joel doing?

Look at this! I've moved the cattle on!

It's that silly sweatband that I don't like

## FINAL STOP

1, 2, 3, off you go Helen...!

And so, after two weeks on the road, we finally reached the end of Turkey. This is the deserted palace of Ishak Pasha, on the old silk trading route, overlooking the modern country of Iran.

As we sat and gazed further into Asia, we thought back to all we'd seen and done. It had been weird, funny, and above all, totally memorable. A road trip we'd never forget.

# OUR TURKEY PHOTO ALBUM
## ONE THOUSAND MILES ACROSS TURKEY, ON THE BEST ROAD TRIP OF OUR LIVES!

Andy was pleased with his entry for the shiniest man in Britain award

Andy's hat was bigger than normal

And so I said, do you want to see my paperclip impression?

You seen my contact lens anywhere?

I think I just found... Andy's contact lens!
Oi, out the way Andy, I can't see the camera!
I should never have given Joel that water pistol!
Nah, this look will never catch on

# ANSWERS AND CREDITS

## BRAIN-PUMPING BLUE PETER (PAGE 9)

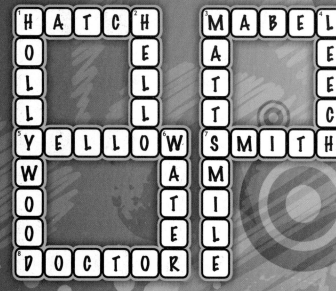

## FINDERS KEEPERS (PAGE 15)

### CLOTHING CONUNDRUM:

1. Joel    2. Helen    3. Andy

4. Helen    5. Andy    6. Joel

### TEAM TALK:

## PUZZLED PETS (PAGES 26-7)

BOWLED OVER: 1. Socks; 2. Shelley; 3. Barney; 4. Lucy. The missing pet is Cookie.

Take the Lead: Helen's got Lucy, Joel's got Mabel and Andy's got Barney.

TRUE OR FALSE: STARTING FROM THE FISH HEAD END: True (Cookie's best friend is Socks); False (Cookie is in fact a boy!); True (Cookie does hate baths); False (Socks actually lives in Hertfordshire); False (Socks does NOT like getting his teeth cleaned); True (Socks is a Ragdoll cat).

## PERSONALITY PROFILES (PAGE 28)

1. Joel; 2. Andy; 3. Helen

## SPOT THE DIFFERENCE (PAGE 42)

## GOLD BADGE WORD SEARCH (PAGE 43)

DANI HARMER: Tracy Beaker actress; DAVID BECKHAM: England footballer and Unicef ambassador; GARY BARLOW: Take That lead singer and organiser of the Comic Relief Kilimanjaro climb; LENNY HENRY: Comedian and face of Comic Relief; LEWIS HAMILTON: Formula 1 world champion 2008; MADONNA: influential female singer; JK ROWLING: Harry Potter author; THE QUEEN: UK head of state; TOM DALEY: world champion diver.